POWER OF YOU

MARK NUSBAUM

The Better Way
GROUP

Power of You

In

The Better Way Series

Website......www.thebetterwaygroup.com/powerofyou

Facebook......www.facebook.com/powerofyoubook

Illustrated by Kaley Doan.

www.kaleyalisondesigns.com

ISBN: 1547248726

ISBN-13: 978-1547248728

All rights reserved.

Including the right of reproduction

in whole or in part in any form.

Copyright © 2017 Mark Nusbaum

FOREWORD

"The fear of the LORD is the beginning of knowledge, but fools despise wisdom and instruction." (Prov. 1:7)

May this book draw you closer to true knowledge about life and leadership.

I am profoundly indebted to my wife, Diane, for her genuine love and support through the years. For the many individuals and teammates with whom I have been privileged to work with through the years---it is your toil, dedication, and sacrifice that are the recipe for producing this book.

May each reader find this book, *Power of You*, to be helpful in becoming a better leader.

CONTENTS

page 7	Introduction
page 11	Power of Early
page 15	Power of Promise
page 18	Power of Givers
page 21	Power of Permission-Based Leadership
page 23	Power of Understanding: Part I
page 28	Power of Understanding: Part II
page 31	Power of Prayer
page 34	Power of Attraction
page 37	Power of Victory
page 40	Power of a Covenant Leader
page 43	Power of Continuous Improvement
page 46	Power of Reflection
page 49	Power of Being Radical
page 52	Power of Now
page 55	Power of Credit
page 58	Power of Desire
page 60	Power of Execution
page 63	Power of Presence
page 66	Power of Precision
page 68	Power of Transformation
page 71	Power of "The Little"
page 74	Power of Thoughtfulness
page 77	Power of Favor

CONTENTS *(cont.)*

page 80	Power of Beauty
page 83	Power of Elimination
page 86	Power of Optimism
page 88	Power of Priorities
page 90	Power of Transparency
page 93	Power of Goal Setting
page 95	Power of Inspiration
page 97	Power of Habits
page 100	Power of Love
page 103	Power of the Problem Solver
page 106	Power of a CEO Mindset
page 109	Power of a Good Great Leader
page 111	Power of Self-Reflection
page 113	Power of Purpose
page 116	Power of the Proverb
page 119	Power of Performance
page 121	Power of Decision
page 124	Power of Presentation
page 128	Power of Accountability
page 132	Power of Contribution
page 136	Power of Ownership
page 139	Power of Lift
page 142	Power of Story
page 144	Power of New Beginnings
page 148	Power of Celebration
page 151	Power of Healing
page 154	Conclusion

INTRODUCTION

This book, *Power of You*, addresses a crisis of leadership that has been unfolding since the 20th century which has affected our politics, marriages, churches, and businesses. Our politicians fight more than lead the country, resulting in scandalous debt and ineffective governance. Our families are falling apart and a large number of marriages are ending in divorce. Churches and synagogues are producing nominal attendance instead of producing world-changing disciples. Businesses are starving for better leaders and scouring the landscape for those who can execute precise game plans without cheating and lying their way to the top.

More consultants, leadership experts, life coaches, seminars, books, articles, and podcasts are thrown at the problem telling us how to lead better. Leadership is synonymous with being successful. If you are a leader, then you are in the business of becoming more successful.

In the 21st century world of unparalleled wealth and technological advancements, Gen X, Gen Y, and Millennial individuals are entering the workforce looking to make their mark in life. They want the "Good Life". They want success. If this means becoming a leader, then so be it. These individuals enter the workforce with a great deal of intelligence, cleverness, and savvy designs about how to live life.

Leadership is supposed to help deliver the Good Life. But the Good Life is strangely hollow and absent amidst the 20 trillion dollar American economy for too many. As millions of smart individuals were led by their talents into leadership positions in the 21st century, the modern day work culture became like a rat race, frenzied for some, and frustratingly unsatisfying for others. How can this be so?

We are informationally driven, techno-centrically efficient, model-based in our thinking. We are organizationally evaluative, employee-centered, and rights-oriented. We have state-of-the art buildings, software, communication systems, and computing power. We have fourth-generation schedules, strategic sales models, cost-cutting outsourcing strategies, and optimized in-housing strategies. Frederick Taylor, a father of early operational and industrial efficiency, would likely marvel at the evolving processes that have created enormous profits.

But something very human has been left behind, it seems. While mastering the art of the deal, tactically getting ahead, and marveling at the shiny new processes, inventions, and trinkets in the marketplace, could we have lost the good foundations that builds quality leaders?

Is it possible we have commoditized good character and put it up for sale like a can of beans? Could the prevailing winds of the day have led us to a moment when everything seems to have a price tag including the selling off of good character for the right price?

Consider students leaving college entering the work force. How many of our students with a diploma in hand find organizations fostering a proud environment of truth, morality, and integrity as the highest order in their culture?

For enough of a promotion, bonus, raise, or recognition, good character easily becomes sacrificial. Good character, once the domain of pre-WWII Puritan America, becomes highly inconvenient when getting the deal done. The salesman, for example, finds himself saying what he thinks he must say to get the deal done. He's not proud of it. His conscience bothers him. But he has a bonus to capture and hyena-like bosses to keep off his back. The board room issues corporate earnings guidance and let's senior managers know that there is a price to pay if mid-level managers, entry level managers, and other employees don't "do what it takes" to capture new business. It's a little like the Godfather in his famous line, "I'm gonna make him an offer he can't refuse."

It seems we have mastered "do what it takes," "the ends justifies the means," and it's "better to ask forgiveness than permission" across the social and leadership spectrum. Ask anyone in the workforce who has worked for a year or more to identify the number of shady practices, outright lies, or inaccurate posturing they have seen. It would hardly surprise most of us to hear these stories of marketplace shenanigans.

The great tragedy of our day is that the higher order of things (soul) are subordinated to primal earthly pursuits. Leadership, under these conditions, is handicapped and cannot synergize and create the best long-term outcomes. Leadership is executed best when soul-ish things of life, *"that which is true, noble, right, pure, lovely, admirable-if anything is excellent or praiseworthy"* (Phil. 4:8), is first among equals in the earthly pursuit of things.

This book, called the *Power of You*, evaluates time-tested attitudes and principles that create long-term sustainable success in the soul and on this earth. The *Power of You* evaluates what good leaders tend to do to succeed both in their character (soul) and on earth (achievements). This process rightfully begins inside-out (soul to achievements) and not outside-in (achievements to soul).

How to Read This Book

The book, *Power of You*, is a vignette of character-based qualities, one-by-one laid out and intended to strengthen and empower leaders. As a mason builds a house brick-by-brick, there is no shortcut in building the good kind of character that translates into good leadership.

The *Power of You* cannot be rushed through. It would be like chug-a-lugging a bottle of honey. Take your time through this read. Your ability, as a leader, to chew and reflect on each quality as it relates to you and identify where you can improve is the key to becoming the best leader you can be. Consider the 3 parts of development the author believes will deliver the best results for the reader:

```
1- Read
2- Reflect
3- Record Thoughts
```

I believe that leaders who employ a measure of courage to reflect, shape, and refine their personal character by absorbing the concept in this book will position themselves for greater influence and long-term success.

With each quality there is a scale of 1 to 10 for you to score yourself. There are designated blank lines for you to write your thoughts after reading each character quality. Write what you believe about yourself in the space provided. Being reflective and transparent are the first steps toward becoming a leader you want to be.

Are you ready to become the leader that defines the norm? Let us begin.

POWER OF EARLY

When you are late, you lose respect.

When you are on time, you are like everyone else.

When you are early, you catch people's attention.

The Power of Early is about delivering yourself, projects, events, and any requirement to others before the time it is due. There are 3 kinds of Leaders:

> 1) Late Arrivers
> 2) On-Timers
> 3) Early Arrivers

Late Arrivers

Every aspiring leader should ask one question:

If I show up late or deliver a project to others after it is due, how many Early Arrivals do I have to do to make up for the Late Arrival in other people's minds?

Ask any employer what he thinks of someone who is late. That employer will say this person either doesn't care, has time management problems, or is inconsiderate of other people's time. **Late Arrivals aren't ready to achieve success at the highest levels.**

If, as a leader, I show up to work late to work one day, how many days do I have to show up early so I can be trusted at the same level again? Maybe I have to show up 5 days early in a row…maybe 8 days….maybe 12 days.

If I have a problem delivering projects early and constantly deliver projects late, will I ever get beyond the level of leadership I am at? Probably not.

As a leader, I shoot myself in the foot every time I deliver myself or my projects late.

If you choose, as a leader, to show up late, you reduce the impact and the effect of everything you say and do. **Late Arrivers don't get promotions, receive a favor, or become elevated very often.** Late Arrivers reduce trust, create animosity, and create friction with others who are trying to perform with excellence.

On-Timers

Leaders who are on time hardly get recognized. Being on time is expected. On-Timers must make a difference in other ways. **Since most people arrive on time or late, this category of people impresses no one.**

There is no excitement about being on time. On-Timers don't inspire or excite others to become better.

Early Arrivers

The only truly prepared people are the early birds. The Power of Early sets you apart as a leader. Being early does three things specifically:

> 1) Prepares you mentally
> 2) Honors others
> 3) Protects your purpose

Prepares you Mentally

Good Leaders who deliver themselves and their projects early have their minds prepared for what must be completed to succeed. There is no substitute for early thinking.

Good Leaders show up early and get a head start over others who don't. **Good Leaders who show up early are more focused and more thoughtful.** They examine matters with greater clarity, intensity, and preparation.

Honors Others

Do you want to show that you care? Show up early. Do it consistently. Make it a habit. You will garner the highest respect before you even begin the task or event you are called for.

Nothing matters to people more than answering one question:

Do you care?

Show up early and you will have earned trust faster because you honor the vision of others around you. Early Arrivers create a sense of urgency. **When you, as a leader, choose to be early, you change the way people think about the project and about you.** That leader is less forgetful and more proactive in nearly all matters.

Protect Your Purpose

Your purpose is built on small victories that turn into larger victories. **It's difficult to have victory during the day when you deliver yourself or your projects late.** Your purpose and destiny are determined by your will to be an Early Arriver.

Only Early Arrivers show themselves approved to take the next step as a leader. **Choose today to be an Early Arriver!**

Question #1:

On a scale from 1 to 10, how well do you employ the Power of Early?

| 1 | 2 | 3 | 4 | 5 | 6 | 7 | 8 | 9 | 10 |

As a leader, describe how much more effective you might be if everything you did was completed early instead of on time:

_____

_____

POWER OF PROMISE

With so many broken marriages, strained work relationships, and lost friendships, is it any wonder why there is so much skepticism regarding promises which are made? Let's note three things about promises:

> 1) Promises made are a dime a dozen.
>
> 2) A promise kept is appreciated.
>
> 3) Promises kept consistently are rare jewels.

Does he mean what he says? What is this person's track record in following through with what he says he will do?

When employees quit working at a place, it's all too often because the actions of others, including the leaders, did not live up to the promise of what was expected. Promises are sacred. They are deeply personal.

The Power of Promise is an underrated but incredibly potent way of living as a leader. Harness the Power of Promise, as a leader, and you will secure the allegiance and loyalty of others in a way that average leaders cannot do. It is the first step toward becoming an unparalleled leader.

There are two types of promises we make as leaders before people:

- Implicit-it's "how" we keep our promise with generosity/cheerfulness.
- Explicit-it's the actual keeping of our promise.

Implicit Promise

Give more than what's expected and complete it earlier than expected. As a leader, learn to live out of generosity and abundance rather than scarcity. This includes a lifestyle of tips at restaurants, words of affirmation, gifts of service, and authentic time-building with others. When you, as a leader, give more and give earlier than expected, you keep an implicit promise. The implicit promise is doing for others more than what is expected, thereby making you an amazing promise keeper. You build a kind of influence in other people's work ethic and their loyalty to the cause.

Explicit Promise

Do what you say you are going to do. People listen and they watch you, even when you don't notice. As a leader, the little things matter. Punctuality, consistency, preparation, etc. are the hallmarks of efficiency; they are spoken and written. Lead by example.

The great exchange between what you say and when another believes what you say is called a promise. It's an IOU! It's a contract. The value of your promise is determined by how quickly you convert that promise to reality! It's not "if" you convert but how quickly.

What do you think of the guy who promises to pay you double the bonus amount if you clean 25 bird cages by 5 pm?

You think, "Great! I'll buckle down! I need the money!"

You finish. The boss man says, "Look, I'm on the other side of town. I'll pay you tomorrow afternoon. Come back and collect your money at that time."

How happy would you be? How highly do you value the promise made by this man? Even if you get paid 24 hours later than you were hoping, the promise of this man has lost a lot of value in your eyes. Maybe next time you won't give it your best or bring the best people out to do the work. The Halo Effect had been tarnished.

Give generously, give early, and give cheerfully. This is the implicit promise that others want from you as a leader. They won't verbalize this, but others respond with fierce loyalty, appreciation, and recognition when you are a unique leader among leaders. **The Power of Promise is, by nature, sacred and deeply personal.** Giving generously, early, and cheerfully will fulfill the deepest belief that others have about you.

Use the Power of Promise well. It opens the door to better relationships, gives you greater purpose, and allows you to excel as a leader. The Power of Promise allows you to become who you want to be!

Question #1:

On a scale of 1 to 10, how well do you use the Power of Promise?

1	2	3	4	5	6	7	8	9	10

Question #2:

As a leader, describe what you can do to improve the Power of Promise in your life.

_____

_____

POWER OF GIVERS

I once asked my dad what the greatest single trait America stood for. Through his eight decades of living, my dad didn't even hesitate to answer. He said, "Generosity."

I found that intriguing. I always grew up believing that Americans were a pretty generous people as a whole. Americans were givers at heart. Americans lived from a position of faith and promise in life as a general rule. We rebuilt Europe with the Marshall Plan, and rebuilt Germany and Japan with American blood and treasure. When catastrophe strikes, Americans seem to be on the scene with resources to help. When you think about American greatness, it often is because Americans have shown the ability to be generous around the globe as a leader of nations.

This idea is also true of individuals. **Individuals are either givers or takers in this world.** These are two competing philosophies about life.

Takers

- Thinks, "Resources are scarce; I better fight to get what I can"
- Lives from a position of fear and insecurity
- Very territorial; driven by holding information from people
- Looks at people as pawns to get ahead instead of building up people
- Fear-Based Living
- Hoard, keep, own, take
- Suspicious of others often; unhappy more than not

Givers

- Invests in others; plants the seed, shares generously
- Lives from a position of faith and promise
- Lives out of an abundance mentality not an attitude of scarcity
- Believes in win-win; lives out win-win
- Faith overcomes and changes the facts
- Shares because it's the right thing to do
- Shares credit, limelight, and the glory
- Considerate; happier more times than not
- Helps others even if they cannot be repaid back
- Wins by bringing others along with him/her

By nature, it's easy to be a taker in life. It's not so easy to be a giver until you decide people matter.

How do people perceive your leadership?

People either see you as a taker or a giver. **You are either a builder of others or you are using others to get what you want.** Aspiring leaders who build others win trust, opportunity, and advancement over time.

When you are a giver of knowledge, time, money, empathy, constructive criticism, encouragement, energy, etc., you build your own destiny. You fulfill your own calling to be the best you can be.

Every aspiring leader has a choice: Giver or Taker---which will you be today?

Question #1:

On a scale of 1 to 10, how much of a giver to others are you?

| 1 | 2 | 3 | 4 | 5 | 6 | 7 | 8 | 9 | 10 |

What can you do to be a greater giver in the lives of others?

_____

_____

POWER OF PERMISSION-BASED LEADERSHIP

The most effective leaders are those who "win permission from others" to lead them. Positional authority takes you only so far. The true respect you earn as a leader comes from knowing how to **"win people's hearts and minds."**

Good leaders also understand that **no one truly gives their consent to be led by others that they don't trust or believe in.** Lower level employees, contractors, mid-level managers, high-level supervisors, and CEO's all have a desire to follow someone they trust and believe in.

What does this kind of trust look like?

"People will only follow you to the extent that they believe in you."

Absorb this thought.

Good leaders authentically **build into** the lives of others with investments of vision, care, time, knowledge, finances, etc. Good leaders, by nature, have been transformed to plant, give, and invest as a matter of lifestyle. They do it, not just because it's the best way to get results, but because it's the right way to live.

Secondly, good leaders don't put a timer on people to get on board the train. They are patient. **Permission-based leadership is a slower, more thoughtful approach to honoring people.** It can take many months to get others to trust you. In fact, the minute a leader chooses to be a permission-based leader, as John Maxwell calls them, he will no longer worry about how much effort or time he should give to those around him. When people around you realize that you are focused on helping them achieve their goals, you will be elevated as a leader.

Lastly, good leaders **harness the power of aligning other people's goals with that leader's objectives.** Good leaders understand how to create win-win scenarios for those who work for them and with them. By winning permission to lead others, those in your sphere of influence will do whatever it takes to help you achieve the larger objective. After all, you have become a person who has found ways to help others grow and become who they want to be.

What are the three basic principles of Permission-Based Leadership previously explained?

---

1) People follow others they believe in.

2) Good leaders don't rush winning permission from others to lead them.

3) Good leaders learn to align the personal and professional goals of others.

Any leader able to live by these principles will likely be exceedingly productive.

Question #1:

On a scale from 1 to 10, how effectively do you win permission to lead others?

| 1 | 2 | 3 | 4 | 5 | 6 | 7 | 8 | 9 | 10 |

As a leader, what specific action steps can you implement to become a better Permission-Based leader?

_____

_____

POWER OF UNDERSTANDING: PART I

Do I understand myself? This is an indispensable key to leading well. If I struggle with what I believe about myself, my future, my present state or about the nature of reality, it means I am human. But until I understand how to answer these questions well, I am limited in my ability to be the best I can be in life.

Key Word: Understanding – "something that you have reason to believe," "a feeling of kindness and caring based on knowledge."

There are two types of leadership views in the world:

> 1) Perennial View of Leadership
> 2) Temporal View of Leadership

Perennial View

- Seek to understand the meaning of life, others, history, money, eternity, higher purpose, and achievement in terms of God.

- People come first as I fulfill my role on earth.

- Lifetime of building others and achieving goals.

- Fixed unchanging moral compass drives my decision-making; moral decisions made based upon what is right, not necessarily what is advantageous to me in the moment.

- The meaning of life is eternal and is born in our hearts and minds.

Temporal View

> - Seek to understand how to achieve the personal results with no thought to God, eternity, or higher purpose.
>
> - Material gain is typically highest priority.
>
> - Attain immediate rewards and the fastest way to get there.
>
> - Use people for my own personal gain.
>
> - Moral decisions made based upon what is advantageous for me in the moment; also known as situational ethics.
>
> - Meaning of life has no permanent value; here today and gone tomorrow.

Leaders become remarkably effective when they "learn the meaning" about who they are as leaders. Then that leader can focus on achieving what is before them.

Am I a Perennial or Temporal Leader?

Let's remember: Both leaders can achieve their objectives in their careers.

In fact, some Temporal Leaders achieve a much larger financial reward for their efforts than Perennial Leaders. But any leader who is being transparent will ask 3 questions of themselves to determine if they are a Temporal or Perennial Leader:

> a) Who Am I?
>
> b) Why Am I Here?
>
> c) Where Am I Going?

Answers from a Perennial Leader

Who Am I?

I am designed with dignity, holiness and purpose. I have been made to know eternity in my heart and to live according to the unchanging, timeless principles of life. The universe and everything in it is finite and has a beginning and will have an end. But the infinite One who created the universe must be responsible for creating me to fulfill my designed purpose on this earth.

Why Am I Here?

Because I am created by the most intelligent, wise and personal Being that created the universe, I will fulfill my purpose with my gifts and talents to love and help others become their best in life.

Where Am I Going?

Because there is an infinite Creator who created me, I will live intentionally knowing that my life is in His hands. I will fulfill my purpose until the final day on earth when His eternal plans will bring me into His Sovereign hands as I take my last breath.

Answers from a Temporal Leader

Who Am I?

Sociologists call me a highly-evolved animal developed through the evolutionary theory. My ancestors were probably apes and I have evolved from single-celled amoebas to what I am today through mutations and random accidents over tens of millions of years.

Why Am I Here?

Cosmic accident with no guiding hand at the helm—not sure there is an overriding purpose for my existence on this earth.

Where Am I Going?

I don't really know—nothing is here to really tell me where I should go or what I should do except what feels right at the moment. I don't know about faith, God, or eternity. I will deal with my situation the best I can.

So, who will you be? Will you be the Perennial or Temporal Leader?

The great teacher, Solomon, wrote in the book of Ecclesiastes 3,000 years ago, that *"[everything] is meaningless, a chasing after the wind," (Ecc. 1:12)* unless you *"remember your Creator in the days of your youth." (Ecc. 12:1)*

Perennial Leaders change the way people think and what they value. They intentionally develop people around them to become better.

Temporal Leaders focus on themselves and how to achieve their goals--maybe making other people better along the way, and maybe not.

The Perennial Leader believes every human life has a destiny, purpose and is meaningful because life is built around eternal purposes. The Temporal Leader believes life is an accident and that purpose, meaning and destiny are words that have no permanent value.

Know who you are. Decide which view of life you hold. Learn to walk decisively so you can lead well and achieve your objectives.

Question #1:

Circle where you are on the Temporal/Perennial scale:

Very Temporal   Very Perennial

| 1 | 2 | 3 | 4 | 5 | 6 | 7 | 8 | 9 | 10 |

Describe two specific things that makes your leadership more temporal or perennial in nature:

(1) _____

_____

(2) _____

_____

POWER OF UNDERSTANDING: PART II

Key Word: Understanding – "something that you have reason to believe," "a feeling of kindness and caring based on knowledge."

When an aspiring leader understands how to help others unleash the purpose for their own lives, that leader will create the power to achieve amazing results.

How do aspiring leaders unleash greatness in others?

> Temporal Needs
>
> Perennial Promises

Aspiring Leaders learn to meet two categories of needs in people's lives:

How many people in your sphere of influence are often afflicted with confusion, failure, doubt, and anxiety? Good leaders understand that their own promises about their future are tied to the success they have in building other people.

If there are no people with problems, then you might as well get in your boat, go to the lake, cast your fishing rod, and enjoy your life. Then repeat this cycle ad infinitum until you die.

Learn the Needs of Others

Who has needs? Everyone does. The CEO, janitor, school teacher, fellow parishioner, stranger on the elevator, workmate, classmate, etc. all have needs. Perennial leaders will choose a life of identifying and meeting the needs of others. Perennial leaders are zealous and persistent about practicing the kind of affection that draws the hearts of others toward the greater purposes of life. Perennial leaders prioritize other people in the battles of life. Whether financial, physical, emotional, spiritual, intellectual, or relational, you as a perennial leader learn where others are weak and have needs. Then, with a listening ear, you honor that person. You meet their needs. You make a lifetime habit of helping others with their frustrations each day. The investment is time, treasure, and talent. It's human capital that matters to the Perennial leader.

Learn the Promises of Others

The aspiring leader believes there is a promise attached to everyone's existence. Everyone has a desire to fulfill their ambitions in life. The question is: How well can you, as a leader, help others facilitate this promise in each person's life? This will determine whether you fulfill your deepest longings and purposes. It will determine your impact.

Maybe it's law school, owning a business, opening a pregnancy center, becoming a coach, firefighter, police officer, counselor, elected official, or military officer-----what can you do and how can you help others with their life's promise?

Aspiring perennial leaders who want to fulfill their purpose in life identify how to fulfill the temporal needs and perennial promises of others.

"And the King will answer them, 'Truly, I say to you, as you did it to one of the least of these my brothers, you did it to me.'" (Matt. 25:40) Meet people where they are in life.

Touch people's lives at the point of their Needs; encourage people at the place of their Promise. By understanding these two leadership principles, you will unleash the greatness of others and fulfill the Perennial Leader in you.

Question #1:

On a scale from 1 to 10, how well do you do meeting the promises and needs of others?

1	2	3	4	5	6	7	8	9	10

How much better does a leader do in the marketplace when that leader works to know the promises and needs of others?

_____

_____

POWER OF PRAYER

The Good Leader who accepts his "High Call" in life sees the source of all that is good, powerful, and purposeful in the Power of Prayer.

A "High Calling" is the belief that **life on earth is driven by a transcendent, eternal, and meaningful higher power.** Life is valuable because it has a "Higher Call". For this reason, the good leader who chooses to accept the "High Call" recognizes and values the Power of Prayer. When centered in the Power of Prayer, a leader's life begins to exhibit a "*Dunamis*" (Greek Word) quality.

We get the words *dynamite*, *dynamo* and *dynamic* from "*Dunamis*".

Dunamis speaks of a miraculous power--**a moral power and excellence of the soul that changes how we live and the way others live.**

This Dunamis Power is born of prayer. Prayer immerses a man in the deepest waters of the soul drawing forth the energies of God into the highest and best use of that man's abilities. In some circles it's called--"being prayed up".

Praying sets "High Call" leaders apart from other leaders.

By beseeching God, the Author of Life, who gives life, purpose, and dignity to all--the "High Call" leader expands who he becomes and avoids growing stale and withering away. This leader is able to impact others at a deeper level of living.

All good leaders are called to fight the good fight. **But good leaders who answer the "High Call" in their own lives, are ones who "move mountains" through the art of praying.** To fight well, they pray first. Then they pray more. These leaders discipline their minds in prayer consistently.

"High Call" leaders understand one thing better than most leaders: Prayer is God's language.

It is the Power of Prayer that fights off worry, depression, destructive lifestyles, physical

debilitation, poor habits, addictions, laziness, and all other ill-temperaments that hinder people's destiny. The Power of Prayer is the tool which reaffirms, re-energizes, and builds who you are to become on this earth.

The "High Call" leader understands prayer doesn't just give you a little bit of peace to get by. The Power of Prayer changes life, health, purpose, relationships, and a leader's vision. The Power of Prayer opens doors and opportunities. The Power of Prayer changes life completely.

With a little seed of faith, the Power of Prayer moves mountains in a leader's life. If you embrace the "High Call" as a leader, you will build your destiny around the ability to take authority of your prayer life. Your children, your boss, your workmates, and everyone in between are better off when a good leader answers the "High Call" of his life to intercede at the deepest levels of existence.

Good leaders with a "High Call" know that life has a way of cutting people up, grinding them up, and destroying the spirit of their life. Life is a spiritual battle as much as it is mental or emotional. The Scripture says the devil comes to "steal, kill, and destroy."

The good leader with a "High Call" knows this, believes this, and uses the Power of Prayer to change the dynamics.

The Power of Prayer builds faith to overcome fear; strength to conquer weakness; joy to evaporate disappointment. Prayer brings encouragement to overcome discouragement. You are nourished with hope in a world that has none. You expand your faith to believe in the possibilities.

The Good Leader who accepts his "High Call" lives by the Scripture that says, *"We are hard pressed on every side, but not crushed; perplexed, but not in despair; persecuted, but not abandoned; struck down, but not destroyed."* (2 Cor. 4:8-9)

Life is messy. And people in the world have contagious problems. But the perennial leader with a "High Call" on his life **will employ the Power of Prayer to change life's**

circumstances. Will you be a superior leader by honoring the "High Call" that touches the lives of others as you are empowered by the Power of Prayer? Will you move mountains and rejuvenate the lives of others you lead? Today, choose how you will serve your short time on earth!

Question #1:

On a scale of 1 to 10, how well do you use the Power of Prayer as a leader to change circumstances?

1	2	3	4	5	6	7	8	9	10

Describe a time when you, as a leader, used prayer as a tool to change a circumstance in your life and was encourage by the choice to do so:

_____

_____

Question #2:

Explain how you can improve and use the Power of Prayer to move mountains in the lives of others you lead:

_____

_____

POWER OF ATTRACTION

You are attracted to those things which you choose to think about. **The more you think about a person, idea, or principle, the greater the attraction will be.** The Power of Attractions is born in the mind.

If as a leader, you want to succeed at the highest level, discipline what you think about. The food you eat, the relationships you think about, the goals you have, the books you read, the workouts you do--**all of these are driven by the Power of Attraction.**

It is a law of nature that you become more of what you think about. Every good leader knows this and begins to **fight for the thoughts** in his mind. **The mind is the battleground that will determine your destiny as a leader.**

Capture and stop the unhealthy thoughts. Poor and unhealthy thoughts randomly may float through your mind. As an aspiring leader, it's your job to see these thoughts when they pop up and say "No...I will not let these thoughts stay here."

Then replace the bad thought with a healthy thought. How do you do this, you may ask? One very simple way:

"Whatever is true, whatever is noble, whatever is right, whatever is pure, whatever is lovely, whatever is admirable—if anything is excellent or praiseworthy—think about such things." (Phil. 4:8)

You may say that this is far too simple. But your choice as a leader is to **think healthily instead of lesser thoughts-- this will determine your destiny and the discipline it takes to get there.**

If you want to achieve your highest potential as a person and as a leader, understand the Power of Attraction and how it works.

There are lots of competing powers of attractions pulling at you and competing for your mind, time, energy, and your destiny. Good leaders know attraction is a blessing.

Attraction tells us we have vitality and desire to "become like" or to "draw close" to those things which are healthy and good.

But to the good leader, who doesn't take the Power of Attraction seriously, and flirts with it to get immediate gratification, the Power of Attraction will metaphorically abuse that person. **Abuse comes when a leader chooses to allow the thoughts of his mind to think upon living in bad relationships, poor food, taking the easy way out in all things, speaking words that are destructive, or taking the path of least resistance.** The Power of Attraction, when abused, destroys who we can become in life.

The Power of Attraction can destroy a good leader or it can take a good leader to the next level toward his destiny. A daily diet of Krispy Kreme is like heaven on earth—but our minds are full of regrets afterward. We took the easy way out. We took the momentary gratification and gave up the long-term goal. A good leader has control over these thoughts and actions. The Scripture says, *"Be transformed by the renewing of your mind."* Romans 12:2

Know your purpose. Understand where you are trying to go. Good leaders know the tension and struggle that comes from the Power of Attraction. The mind and heart will compete for every decision a leader makes.

Choose this day to be attracted to *"whatever is noble, excellent, pure, admirable, or praiseworthy"* (Phil. 4:8) which are the right things in life so that you may live well and become the leader you are called to be.

Question #1:

On a scale from 1 to 10, I am attracted to choices that avoid immediate gratification and allow me to become who I want to be.

1	2	3	4	5	6	7	8	9	10

What specifically can you do to be attracted to the things that will make you a better leader instead of an average leader?

_____

_____

POWER OF VICTORY

Key Word: Victory - "the act or an example of winning a competition or war."

Victory generates hope. It brings life alive today, and it generates enthusiasm. Victory creates momentum and confidence. It creates a new image. Victory creates awe. Victory facilitates trust, and victory raises belief. Victory makes the impossible more possible. Victory makes our destiny more interesting, hopeful, and attractive.

Victory is oxygen. It gives life and meaning to the effort you put into the goals you set. Goals worth pursuing are arduous, time-consuming, and have many twists and turns that includes frustration before you ever taste the sweet part of victory.

Even though you can become a powerful CEO, Dentist, District Attorney, Elected Official, Doctor, Veterinarian, or any other noble occupation, **breaking this long road down into smaller parts is vital to a leader's success.** As a leader, make a promise to yourself that you can keep. **Every promise you keep to yourself, no matter how small, is a victory.** Start with little things that can be victories. Little things could include:

- Make a promise to have your bed made each day before leaving the house.
- Making sure the dishes are clean before going to bed.
- Having the car clean each time you leave the car in the driveway.
- Making sure you are early to work each and every day.
- Making sure to study something valuable each day of the week for 15 minutes.

Every aspiring leader has something to work on. It doesn't matter who they are. **The critical key is to decide that you, as a leader, will have enough "little victories" that prove to yourself you are trustworthy enough to have big victories.**

Aspiring leaders, who have talent, will and desire sometimes sputter and spin their wheels while other leaders steadily move higher in responsibility, compensation, and opportunity. Why?

The difference always starts with being faithful with keeping your promise to have small victories. It's getting to work early. It's keeping your promises to yourself that make you who you are to become. It's finding a way to honor the other person regardless of their conduct. When you keep your promises to yourself daily, you are creating small victories. **No matter how little or insignificant, victories change the way a leader sees life and grows.**

Victory generates hope. It brings life alive today. It generates enthusiasm. Victory creates momentum. Victory creates confidence, and it creates a new image. Victory creates awe, facilitates trust, and raises belief. Victory makes the impossible more possible. Victory makes our destiny more interesting, hopeful, and attractive to us and to others.

Live better today. Achieve success in little things that create victory for you. By doing so, the big victories become reachable and tangible.

Question #1:

On a scale from 1 to 10, how well do I string small victories together each day?

1	2	3	4	5	6	7	8	9	10

What can you do to improve the number of victories you have as a leader?

_____

_____

Question #2:

What daily promise can you make to yourself so that you can create victory through that one promise?

_____

_____

POWER OF A COVENANT LEADER

Covenant Leader or Contract Leader?

Covenant Leader

> Permanent-Honors others always
>
> Personal-Relational in nature
>
> Promise-Authentic vision for others

Contract Leader

> Temporary - Honors others for a time
>
> Impersonal - Transactional in nature
>
> Limited Promise - Situationally driven

Your leadership can take one of two paths with others. You can be a Covenant Leader or a Contract Leader.

Covenant Leader

A Covenant Leader is one who decides to honor each person with a permanent-personal promise regardless whether this person can advance the Covenant Leader's life or not. The Covenant Leader supports you because they choose to believe in you and what you can become. **The Covenant Leader has decided in advance that every single person they encounter during the day matters.** The Covenant Leader invests time, energy and money to grow other people. **The goal of the Covenant Leader is to**

leave each person better off than before they met. They employ human capital toward everyone as a lifestyle.

The Covenant Leader doesn't decide to withhold words of blessing or acts of assistance. Covenant Leaders are generous. They do the following consistently:

- Plant seeds
- Meet needs
- Create value
- Give generously
- Become relevant

Contract Leader

The Contract Leader seeks to achieve an immediate objective. They treat people well enough to achieve the goal. But they believe that people are dispensable. Their relationships are transactional; not relational. It's all about "what you can do for me now."

The Contract Leader doesn't work through people's problems. People should solve their own problems. Investing in the lives of others is expensive, time-consuming, and often won't pay off. The Contract Leader will invest time in people they believe will improve their own careers, status, or position. The Contract Leader gives under the condition they receive something of value in return. Contract Leaders create value for themselves, but only create value in another person if that person is first valuable to the Contract Leader.

Contract Leaders and Covenant Leaders can both achieve short-term objectives in their personal lives and professional lives. Covenant Leaders do, however, build out an ever-increasing network of influence among others when Contract Leaders will have difficulty doing so. The Covenant Leader leads with a permanent, personal promise which focuses on bringing dignity and vision to the lives of each person they encounter.

Question #1:

On a scale of 1 to 10, how much do you think others perceive you as a Covenant Leader?

| 1 | 2 | 3 | 4 | 5 | 6 | 7 | 8 | 9 | 10 |

What does a Covenant Leader so differently than a Contract leader in the marketplace that is attractive for those being led?

_____

_____

POWER OF CONTINUOUS IMPROVEMENT

Nearly everyone in business wants to lead better. But many CEO's, Managers, and Vice-Presidents don't have clarity on what it means to do so. Most leaders know that if they were better leaders, the organization would perform better. Their teams would manage time, resources, and people better which delivers greater results.

There are 5 specific areas Aspiring Leaders can work to become better:

> 1) Self-Awareness: "How I Come Across to Others"
>
> 2) Self-Management: "The Ability to Restrain my Impulses"
>
> 3) Others: "Recognize the Needs of Others"
>
> 4) Relationships: "The Ability to Adapt"
>
> 5) Don't Let Things Come Out Sideways

Self-Awareness: "How I Come Across to Others"

How do others perceive my leadership? Am I perceived as disorganized, disheveled, a talker, a time-waster, and a minimalist? Or do others perceive me as an encourager, a doer, an achiever, and one who can be trusted with people and processes?

It is possible to achieve your organizational objectives but go no higher in an organization. You hit an invisible ceiling. Why? Because some leaders who may be really good at what they do don't have a keen enough "self-awareness" about the signals they send to those with whom they work. That leader gets frustrated. They have achieved their objectives. But they don't seem to have the next step ready for them to advance.

All leaders should look in the mirror and ask, "How am I improved by others"?

It matters.

Self-Management: "The Ability to Restrain my Impulses"

How many leaders excel in their work ethic and deliver superior results? Yet, these leaders limit their own growth in an organization because they fail to "restrain their impulses". Instead of managing circumstances well, that leader may blow off some steam and burst out in a fit of anger. Maybe that leader decides to talk about others behind the scenes (gossip). Maybe that leader chooses to go home, giving in to being tired instead of completing everything that should be finished that day. Regardless of the area where a leader chooses to act out of their impulses, **that leader is saying to others that they aren't ready for the next step in the organization.**

Others: "Recognize the Needs of Others"

How many times are people an "It" when conducting business? Leaders who treat others like pawns on a chess board may still succeed in their business venture. But they typically won't succeed with the same people they started with. **When you meet the needs of others, they will perform much better for you and the organization as a rule of thumb.** The difficulty in meeting the needs of others is that it requires time, energy, and sometimes money. None of this is written out in a leader's job description. But those few leaders who understand how people work and how to live life well, will not "use" others. But that leader will inspire and empower everyone around him/her. Why? Because it's the right way to live.

Relationships: "The Ability to Adapt"

Leaders who are inflexible lose good people. Often times, they don't understand why they have turnover. Knowing how to relate well requires knowing what your people are going through. It requires knowing what inspires them. It requires knowing how to grow others.

The leader who makes work simply a transaction or a paycheck will often fail to grow

others and deliver superior results at the end of the day. When a leader is able to learn how to connect to a wide variety of people around them, that leader has a chance to win. Adapting to where others are is about honoring those around you while working toward achieving set goals.

Don't Let Things Come Out Sideways

It takes only one sentence from a leader that comes out wrong to destroy trust with others. Human capital begins with an authentic and consistent design to build others. In a moment of stress, difficulty, or frustration, delivering bad body language or inappropriate comments will distract others from doing their work at best. At worst, it may derail others for a long period of time from growing or achieving the organization's goals. Let each word be a platform to build others in their quest to fulfill their destiny.

Question #1:

On a scale of 1 to 10, how well are you focused on continuous improvement?

1	2	3	4	5	6	7	8	9	10

What one habit can you change to become a leader that continuously improves?

_____

_____

POWER OF REFLECTION

Think about who you are. Who do others think you are? Why others think you are who you are?

This is reflection.

There are 3 kinds of reflections important to aspiring leaders:

> 1) Reflection of Self
> 2) Reflection of Others
> 3) Reflection of Circumstances

Self-Reflection

Who am I? Who do I want to be? Being self-aware of who you are and who you want to be is critical to growing as a person and a leader.

When you reflect on self, you have a chance to grow. It's easy to be distracted by being busy and not thinking about who you are and who you want to be on a regular basis. But by being an active agent in pursuit of your goals, you should be aided by reflection- it is essential. **You are not a machine. You are a human being with amazing capacity to grow and develop.**

Just like a bodybuilder who trains his body into shape, he will take protein to rebuild the torn down muscles. Without protein, a bodybuilder cannot build his muscles and become something better.

Reflection for an aspiring leader is protein. Reflection is the building block of growth and leadership. To lead well, a leader must reflect well.

Reflecting on Others

Reflect on why others see you the way they do. What others think of you may not be exactly true. But there is a kernel of truth that leads others to believe what they believe about you.

Choose to have a high standard of moral clarity and conduct for yourself, but learn to accept where others are in their life's journey. **Reflect on how you can build others up in their journey professionally and personally.**

Choose not to brood with anger over others because they have acted against you or selfishly ignored you. Understand that people often act out of fear and insecurity when dealing with others. Instead, learn how to consistently meet the needs of others. Listen to those around you. Talk less. **Learn how each person receives affirmation differently and become a superior advocate for that person. Learn how to help others succeed where they struggle.**

Reflecting on Circumstances

Circumstances are the testing road. Can you handle circumstances and make life better for those around you? Circumstances are life's way of testing your ability to succeed. If you reflect well on who you are and who you want to be, and if you reflect on how to meet the needs of others so that they succeed at the highest level, **circumstances won't determine your destiny.** You will likely convert bad circumstances into good circumstances.

Why is this so? Because you, as an aspiring leader, have chosen to consistently reflect on who you want to be and how to make others better in life.

Reflect today. Make it part of your daily habit!

Question #1:

On a scale of 1 to 10, how well do you use the Power of Reflection to become better?

| 1 | 2 | 3 | 4 | 5 | 6 | 7 | 8 | 9 | 10 |

Explain how the Power of Reflection improves your ability to lead others:

_____

_____

POWER OF BEING RADICAL

Key Word: Radical - "causing or being an example of great change; extreme."

Good leaders stand out and succeed when they learn to be radical in the right areas of leadership.

To be **"different from the usual or traditional" is a mark that separates an effective leader from others.** Radical, in leadership terms, means to be determined, sold out, focused, undeterred, resolute, unwilling to lose, etc., in specific areas.

Good leaders should be radical in three areas:

> 1) Truthful Living
>
> 2) Growing Others
>
> 3) Executing Game Plans

Truthful Living

Authenticity is the key to becoming who you want to become. Don't cut corners. Don't cheat. Don't lie. When you do, admit it. Confess it. Make it right. Choose to grow and become better.

You can never be an admired and respected leader by believing you should cut corners because everyone else does. Leaders can make money skimming off the top, hiding the truth and playing games with others. But leaders won't get the best out of others or win hearts and minds by cutting corners. Money is a poor motivational substitute for becoming who you want to become. Better leaders become radical about virtues that create superior character.

You should learn your weaknesses and your strengths and **become radical about**

building the virtues of good character each moment of the day. Good leaders look in the mirror. They constantly ask if they are living what is true and right as a matter of character.

Growing Others

Every leader has objectives to accomplish. **Better leaders learn to grow others with authority and vision,** that they may excel and succeed. Become radical about growing others. Those influenced by you will be more empowered to help you achieve stated goals.

Be different from the usual or traditional leaders you see. Become radical about learning who the people around you are. Become radical about learning what makes them tick. **Be radical about channeling the energy of others** and focus toward meeting their own personal and professional goals. Be radical about inspiring those around you to become better each day.

Radical commitment to others can be exhausting. But it is the highest form of investment. When you consistently pour into other people's lives, you become the leader you are supposed to be.

Executing Game Plans

Your goal as an inspiring leader is to achieve the stated objectives before you. Game plans are broken down into goals which are further broken down into tasks. Tasks require intelligent use of personnel and resources. **Becoming radical and unusually focused on employing people and resources urgently maximizes people's abilities.** Using your relational skills, demand to know why projects aren't being completed faster or with excellence. **Be radical about urgency. Be radical about demanding the most from those around you.** Be radical about giving the most and best of your effort and time. Be radical about giving credit and authentic praise to those around you when they deserve it.

Every minute counts. Every project counts. Every goal counts. Becoming radical about maximizing people's talent and their time. **By holding the team and individuals accountable to specific performance measures, you become radical.** You don't accept less. You honor others along the way. You recognize each person's abilities that help them achieve the most. This is how you gain leadership credibility.

Being radical is about caring about what matters—the truth, growing others, and executing the game plan!

Question #1:

On a scale from 1 to 10, how radical are you about:

The Truth:

| 1 | 2 | 3 | 4 | 5 | 6 | 7 | 8 | 9 | 10 |

Growing Others:

| 1 | 2 | 3 | 4 | 5 | 6 | 7 | 8 | 9 | 10 |

Executing the Game Plan:

| 1 | 2 | 3 | 4 | 5 | 6 | 7 | 8 | 9 | 10 |

Explain:

_____

_____

POWER OF NOW

Yesterday is gone, and tomorrow is not promised to us. The present time is all that matters. It is in the "Now" that aspiring leaders excel. They use the "Now" Moments to determine their destiny.

Every leader must determine to live the "Now" moment well or to squander it forever. "Now" is currency, which exists in the present moment; not yesterday, or tomorrow.

In life, we have 657,000 "Now" hours equating about 75 years to live. Good leaders spend it well.

Whether rich or poor, each hour must be spent one at a time. There is no advantage. The rich man has no more time than the poor fellow. The wise man has little more time than the fool.

The difference is what we build with the "Now" Moments in our midst. Will we use them to create something of perennial value? Or will we exchange them for something temporal--something far less than everything the soul says we need?

The "Now" Moments change our destiny through the way we:

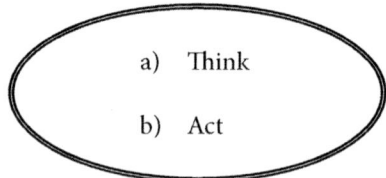

<u>Think</u>

In an attempt to be a Good Leader, I will not let "Now" Moments go by. I will not think miserably and poorly of other people or with an impoverished mindset about my purpose. Every time I mindfully dismiss, dishonor or disdain another person, I will have lost the "Now" Moment to align that person with his/her destiny. As a leader, I will not waste each "Now" Moment thinking in particular ways that destroy the purposes of my life. My "Now" Moments tell me I have destiny and purpose.

Act

I will employ my "Now" Moments zealously to act with vision and servant-hood for others to meet their temporal needs (earthly & physical) and their perennial needs (promises & purpose). **Only my "Now" Moments allows me to grow, become, achieve, and have victory in life.** So, I will act with the greatest care in each "Now" Moment to invest time, energy, and money in the lives others as well as mine.

Victory for my life happens "Now"; not tomorrow, not yesterday.

The power of "Now" is that it alone changes our destiny. It is our currency, the "Now" Moment, that makes us wealthy. **It is the "Now" currency that allows us to become "who" we are to be and "what" we are to accomplish.**

Good Leaders believe there is something remarkably valuable, beautiful, and precious about "Now" moments. Each "Now" moment invested doesn't just ebb away and evaporate. Like a professional masonry job, **each metaphorical brick is an hour of life laid down carefully and skillfully.**

This is the way a Good Leader builds his perennial mansion in the sky, one metaphorical brick after another. The compilation of "Now" Moments upon "Now" Moments is the **Good Leader's way of dignifying the life of others and fulfilling the purpose of that leader's destiny**--a destiny not bound by earthly time.

Christ Jesus spent his "Now" Moments on earth building the heavenly mansions for those whose hearts would trust Him. *"There is no greater love than to lay down one's life for his friends."* (John 15:13)

Will we, as leaders, use the "Now" Moments to lay our lives down for others to fulfill our highest call on this earth?

Question #1:

On a scale from 1 to 10, how well do you use your "Now" moments?

1	2	3	4	5	6	7	8	9	10

Why does the Power of Now become a valuable concept to leaders who aspire to maximize their potential?

_____

_____

POWER OF CREDIT

Good leaders learn how and when to deliver credit and recognition to others. To be recognized means to get credit. When others receive credit from a leader, it's a highly satisfying moment.

Credit and recognition is like oxygen. They are essential to the lifeblood of people and organizations. When you, as a leader, give authentic credit about another's performance, you create an amazing array of benefits:

> 1) Truthful Living
>
> 2) Growing Others
>
> 3) Executing Game Plans

Leaders who are stingy or slow in recognizing and delivering credit in their organizations create an atmosphere of low morale, a thin veneer of loyalty, and an uninspired workforce. Absenteeism, inattention to results, and a lack of accountability and trust are only some of the challenges facing leaders who are not intentional about delivering credit in a timely manner.

A good leader who delivers credit does two important things:

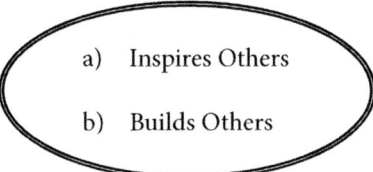

Inspire Others

Leaders who tap into the deepest desires of those around them are the ones that create better outcomes. No organization, no relationship, and no individual becomes better in life until they are first inspired to become better. Delivering credit is an inspirational exercise. **The leader who employs the Power of Credit wisely unlocks the desire in others to become even better and take ownership of their actions and the results of their actions.**

Many people around you will do their job. But how many will deliver a superior performance without receiving credit for the good work they do? Credit, when delivered to those who earn it, inspires them to become even better at what they do.

Building Others

Leaders who share credit build stronger organizations. Leaders who take credit create insecurity and jealousy. **The Law of Credit states that everyone wants recognition for the work they put out.**

Leaders who understand this law and employs it with others properly, excel at higher levels. **The leader who does not share credit very easily is actually stealing what rightfully belongs to others.** That leader will not be trusted nor be liked.

The leader, who quickly and thankfully delivers credit in public for the work others have completed, will grow others around him.

Credit is a powerful nutrient in life. People act or don't act based upon whether they will receive credit. Money alone does not determine how effective people will be. It's knowing the impact of your work and your significance that drives people to create excellent results.

Good leaders are good by definition because they don't hoard credit that doesn't belong to them. Good leaders share credit generously. They recognize the value others bring to the table.

As an inspiring leader, do your words and actions inspire and build others around you? You will know by the effort and results that you get from others.

Question #1:

On a scale from 1 to 10, how generous are you in delivering credit to others?

| 1 | 2 | 3 | 4 | 5 | 6 | 7 | 8 | 9 | 10 |

As a leader, if you could improve giving credit to others more freely, what one attitude would you have to change to do so?

_____

_____

POWER OF DESIRE

Key Word: Desire - "a strong feeling of wanting something."

Desire is the key to fueling achievement. Greater desire means greater opportunity that an individual will have to deliver superior results. Three things about desire should be noted:

1) Desire is naturally **amorphous**. Desire has **no boundaries**. Water finds its way anywhere and destroys anything in its path because by nature it has no boundaries. Desire acts the same way. Desire has no moral compass by itself. Smart leaders recognize this idea. **The power of desire can destroy who we want to be.** Just ask married couples who divorce because desire overwhelmed one of the individuals. Or people who steal because the desire to have something overwhelmed them. Because desire is amorphous by nature, it can destroy a leader's future unless that leader takes specific care concerning the power of desire.

2) Desire should be **channeled properly**. Suppressing desire is like killing who we are. That's not the answer to living well as a leader. **Desire is like lighter fluid.** It's a fuel. If channeled properly, desire can drive us to the highest levels of achievements. But because desire is **amoral** and has no intrinsic restrictions upon itself, good leaders understand how to focus their efforts directing their immense desire and energy upon specific visions and goals.

3) Desire is best channeled by **strong character.** Vision and goals are not strong enough to channel desire properly. Strong character is necessary to channel desire properly. Strong character presupposes right thinking and actions. Remember that right thinking and right actions are not natural or normal qualities. **Right thinking and right actions are developed through daily struggles.** Put enough of these daily struggles together and we will now have created some good habits. Strong character is the sum of your good habits which comes from right thinking

and right actions. Strong character can now channel the power of desire to its better end as a leader without destroying others around you in the process.

Good habits are the key to strong character. With strong character (right thinking and right actions), the power of desire will be channeled to a leader's greater purpose, their destiny. That leader will employ the power of desire to achieve goals and visions that otherwise would remain unattainable.

<u>Question #1:</u>

On a scale from 1 to 10, how well, as a leader, do you channel your desires toward successful outcomes instead of destructive ones?

1	2	3	4	5	6	7	8	9	10

How well do you use the Power of Desire to execute and achieve your goals in a timely way?

_____

_____

POWER OF EXECUTION

Key Word: Execution - "the act of doing or performing something in a planned way."

Effective Leaders who excel execute game plans at the highest level. Leaders who don't execute well are ones who often fail to meet their strategic goals and fail to remain leaders. What exactly are the differences which distinguish between leaders who execute the game plan well and those who do not?

Clear Game Plan

Know exactly what has to be accomplished and when. It's sounds simple. But effective leaders rarely mistake the "what" that has to be completed. Effective leaders envision the end game. **They see what the achievement should look like before the achievement happens.** Effective leaders don't let circumstances overwhelm or cloud their vision about what will happen.

Implement Resources

Just like a successful football coach who evaluates and learns which athlete plays better at each position on the field, a leader who is effective does the same thing in his organization. Leaders realize they have money, budget, personnel, and strategies. **Learning to implement the combination of resources that will maximize performance is what effective leaders do better than others.**

Inspire Achievement

Is it possible for leaders to have superior talent and not achieve the strategic goals? Absolutely!

Effective leaders inspire achievement by employing the soft skills to make the chemistry of their team better. They understand how to create order and vision as well as get the most out of their talented team members. Executing the game plan requires an effective leader to use the soft skills of leadership. **Included in the soft skills is some**

understanding of psychology, human nature, momentum, and inspiration.

What inspires people to succeed at the highest levels of their capabilities? This is what effective leaders spend their lives learning. Because executing the game plan means getting others to think and act with exceptional zeal and competence.

Perseverance

If leading effectively was easy, everyone would have a gold star. But it's not easy for many reasons stated above. **Maybe the greatest trait of effective leaders is that they simply don't quit even when circumstances are really tough.** Deadlines, shortage of funds, extra time needed after hours, and failure by others that affect you are only some of the constant challenges.

But an effective leader employs a sense of tenacity commitment, energy level, urgency, and creativity that doesn't slow down. The effective leader raises the bar for performance so others can see what that leader expects. The effective leader doesn't radiate doubt about the game plan or the worthiness of the project being completed in front of others. The effective leader never acts with laziness or creates bad shortcuts when executing the game plan. Instead, the effective leader will work harder as a general rule and demand excellence in all of the details of the game plan.

Summary

Leaders who see a clear game plan, implement their resources well, inspire achievement in others, and persevere are effective leaders. Why are these leaders effective? Because these are the leaders who execute the game plan well on a consistent basis.

Question #1:

On a scale from 1 to 10, how well do you use the Power of Execution to succeed at the highest level?

| 1 | 2 | 3 | 4 | 5 | 6 | 7 | 8 | 9 | 10 |

What one obstacle regularly gets in the way from you executing your game plans and meeting your goals?

_____

_____

POWER OF PRESENCE

Presence is the idea of being here. To have "presence" has two different meanings for aspiring leaders:

> 1) To be "Physically Present" to make sure goals are achieved.
>
> 2) To be "Transcendentally Present" so that goals are achieved.

Do you have to be a leader who is "Physically Present" or can you be "Transcendentally Present" to achieve your goals? These two ideas about presence will ultimately determine how far you can go as a leader.

Leaders who rely on being "Physically Present" to supervise every detail of their team may win in the short-term. But "Physically Present" leaders lose long-term in two specific ways:

> 1) Drained of their energy supervising details of others.
>
> 2) Drained of their time that should be put toward better tasks.

You need energy and time to become a better leader and go after larger goals. Even though "Physically Present" leaders may be proud of their immediate accomplishments, they struggle to achieve objectives beyond what they can't immediately and directly control. Their influence is limited.

"Transcendentally Present" leaders are ones who don't have to be physically present to get others to achieve their goals. Transcendentally Present Leaders are those who win hearts and minds. They build and invest in others in very specific ways.

The impact of a "Transcendent Presence" is so powerful that it doesn't matter if this leader is in the room or not. The teammates with whom they work are loyal to the cause because they have been invested in it. The team members are focused with entrepreneurial value to achieve the stated objectives. Team members become the best leaders they can be as a result when they are invested in it.

The Good Leader who is "Transcendentally Present" can maximize time:

> 1) Focusing on planning and developing dreams and goals.
>
> 2) Focusing on planning and developing the higher-level strategies necessary to become and achieve what you want.

If people around you complete their work with excellence only when your eye is on them, then that is a sign that you are a "Physically Present" Leader. **If people around you complete their work with excellence when you are not in their presence, then that is a sign that you are a "Transcendentally Present" Leader.**

Why do teachers all across the country stay in the classroom while students take tests? It's because students are not in a place where they have been "Transcendentally" impacted. **It should be noted that when a student is impacted by "Transcendental Presence" of a mentor, parents, coach, God, or another role model, they will likely not need the "Physical Presence" of a teacher in the room while that student takes the test.** That student becomes a better, more trusted person who is on the path toward good character and good leadership.

As companies grow larger, why do they add a greater number of supervisors? Isn't it often because without supervisors that work performance decreases? If you, as an aspiring leader, are able to reach the hearts and minds of people around you, will your physical presence be required as much? Probably not.

There is only one substitute for physical presence to drive better performance for you and your organization. It's called "Transcendence Presence".

Do you have transcendent presence? When your ideas, example, and influence creates a serious impact on others, you will have achieved a "Transcendent Presence" as a leader.

Question #1:

On a scale from 1 to 10, how well does your leadership reflect transcendental presence?

1	2	3	4	5	6	7	8	9	10

Describe whether your leadership presence today is more temporal or transcendental. Explain:

_____

_____

POWER OF PRECISION

How precise is your leadership?

Have you wondered why some things have a beauty to them? A certain sort of perfection?

Answer: Precision.

Key Word: Precision - "the quality of being exact."

Why do people want to purchase the Audi, BMW, and Lexus car series? The precision of these vehicles – the way they drive, the way they feel, and the accuracy of the way they handle the road is understood by anyone who gets behind the wheel. If you have driven a Ford Pinto and then stepped into one of these luxury cars, you never want to go back to the Ford Pinto.

Precision has a certain beauty, elegance and exactness about it. There are lots of things in life that are functional, but not many things are precise. **There is no question as to why the product or service you are enamored with is so valuable. It's because of the approach to perfection it represents.**

Precision occurs only when you have:

---

1) Unrelenting Effort (Sweat & Tears)

2) Unstoppable Desire to Succeed (Time, Practice, Practice, Practice)

3) Repeat Focus (Again and Again)

As an example, you can purchase a handmade Swiss watch of which there are very few in the marketplace. You can pay up to $500,000. Why? Because it's so precisely made with exactness of millisecond time-keeping that makes the watch remarkable and a beautiful piece of machinery.

This is true for everything in life. Diamonds, baseball card collections, paintings, music, muscle building, and yes---even leadership.

Precision is about perfecting your craft toward the marvel of perfection.

If you aspire to be the highest and best performing leader, precision must be about how you operate. Precision means being knowledgeable about every detail, executing every detail, and demanding excellence from every detail in your control.

What are you so precise about in your leadership that you deliver the kind of results that changes the way people think about you?

There are 5 areas you should be remarkably precise in to succeed at the highest level:

Question #1:

On a scale of 1 to 10, how committed are you to be a Leader of Precision?

1	2	3	4	5	6	7	8	9	10

What do you appreciate about the Power of Precision from a leadership perspective?

_____

_____

POWER OF TRANSFORMATION

Your destiny is determined by how much you choose to submit to the Power of Transformation. No one is born a great leader. Leaders are developed. When you see a good leader, you don't see all the shaping, changing, training, pain, learning, and developing. You see and enjoy the fruit of these transformative years.

How do you start to deliberately submit to the Power of Transformation?

Saint Paul in the Scripture says, *"Do not conform to the pattern of this world, but be transformed by the renewing of your mind. Then you will be able to test and approve what God's will is—his good, pleasing and perfect will."* (Romans 12:2)

> Trans = across, beyond, or through
>
> Form = the figure or shape of something

Key Word: Transform - "to change completely the appearance or character of someone."

> 1) Desire to become better.
> 2) Schedule time to become better.
> 3) Follow through with the schedule.

Desire

Nothing substitutes for the innate hunger to want to become better. **The leader who understands that his destiny is all about loving the journey of becoming better will be an overcomer of obstacles.** Life has a way of keeping you right where you are. Things that are stationary tend to stay stationary. But it doesn't have to be this way.

Desire is born from inspiration about thinking, reading, learning, and developing the mind and heart to see and love what you should become through the Power of Transformation. **When good desire that aligns with what is true and right, nearly all things are possible.**

Schedule Time

Deliberately learn. **Deliberately set aside time daily to absorb ideas and material. Deliberately spend time contemplating God, purpose, destiny, and transforming of your spirit, soul, and body.** If you are not deliberate, you will stunt your growth as a leader. The Power of Transformation is not automatic. The Power of Transformation is born by voraciously setting aside time to become better. Life has a way of lulling all of us to sleep. Too often, it makes us comfortable with where we are. **This is the enemy of transformation.**

Maybe it's the bookstore. Maybe it's the coffee shop and YouTube videos. Maybe it's formal education. The act of your will, as a leader, to schedule transformation invites the Power of Transformation to do its work in you. **To transform means you, as a leader, should deliberately schedule the right amount of time to be transformed.**

Follow Through

You will be tired. There will be bills. You might be overwhelmed, hungry, underpaid, unhappy, over-worked, unprepared---lots of excuses exist to not follow through with the Power of Transformation. These will be the reasons some leaders will not go beyond the current shape or figure they are in.

The leaders who succeed at higher levels **succeed at keeping their little commitments** to growing, showing up, and not quitting on training the mind, body, and soul.

To go beyond the current shape or figure you are in requires dedicated unrelenting decision that you will **schedule and follow through** with the Power of Transformation. The most effective leaders don't burn themselves out in life. Good leaders renew themselves through the reflective Power of Transformation.

Be reminded of the effects the Power of Transformation has on your life:

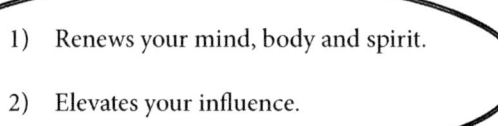

1) Renews your mind, body and spirit.
2) Elevates your influence.

Let's be clear. **The Power of Transformation is about forward scheduling how you are going to become better and maximize your destiny.**

Question #1:

On a scale from 1 to 10, how well do you submit to the Power of Transformation to become a better leader?

1	2	3	4	5	6	7	8	9	10

What one concrete step can you take today to allow the Power of Transformation to make you a better leader?

_____

_____

POWER OF "THE LITTLE"

Can a leader rise to a sustained level of significant influence if the little things in his life are not completed with excellence? **How can God trust you with big things if little things are not met with excellence?**

Little things are the testing ground to see if you can handle great things. It starts with how early or late you show up to work. Do you work smart or do you just work hard? Do you work in such a way to honor others around you? Do others see themselves better because you have built into their lives? Have you learned to complete your tasks in a timely way? If not, have you grown in your ability to delegate tasks and grow others in the process?

Do you tend to give reasons for why protocols and procedures aren't followed? Do you create organizational and administrative order wherever you are? Or do you feel like you are flying by the seat of your pants? Do you know how to say the right thing at the right time in order to deliver "win-win" scenarios? **When people walk into your presence, do they recognize order, fairness, and leave better off than when they entered your presence?**

These are little things. But these little things add up every moment of every day to create your destiny!

Good Leaders become superior because they live by an unchangeable moral code:

> 1) Do what is right because it is right.
> 2) Do it early, not late.
> 3) Do it with exceptional human capital to deliver a superior performance.

One of the major differences between Good Leaders who live by an unchangeable moral code and average leaders is this:

Quality Control

All the examples earlier have a quality control element to them. You can do them well consistently, or you can do them poorly. It's your choice as a leader.

Anybody can deliver a product to the marketplace. But not everyone will deliver the "highest and best" quality to the customer. **The difference between the Good Leader and the average leader is often found in quality control.** The Good Leader will not let the food, apartment, vehicle, or any other service be delivered without demanding excellence in the product.

Quality control takes lots of effort. It takes sweat. It takes time. Good Leaders go to war against laziness and fatigue. They know that laziness and fatigue keep them from being the best Quality Control Experts they can be. Good leaders choose not to pretend that everyone is doing what they are supposed to "because it's their job."

Good leaders learn to review, double check, and inspire their team to go back, fix it, clean it, and make it better—the next time they have an opportunity, they do it right the first time. Good leaders are relentless in their pursuit of Excellent Quality.

Those leaders who live for Quality Control checks and demand the service be excellent in the office and the product be excellent have an opportunity to be Good Leaders!

It's the little things—the clean windows, the clean office, the professional dress, the voice on the phone, the organization of the presentation, the excellence of the product, and the timeliness of seasoned words that grows leaders into their destiny.

There are no shortcuts. Little things grow into big things. Good little habits become great big habits.

When "little things become great" it's because Quality Control becomes the relentless pursuit of a Good Leader.

Question #1:

On a scale from 1 to 10, how important is the Power of Little in your life?

| 1 | 2 | 3 | 4 | 5 | 6 | 7 | 8 | 9 | 10 |

How can you better employ the Power of Little in your life to achieve your goals?

_____

_____

POWER OF THOUGHTFULNESS

Good leaders are thoughtful leaders. It takes time. It takes energy. And it is person-specific. It is the highest honor to receive the time and thought of another person.

Thoughtfulness is knowing what to say, when to say it, what to give, when to give it—it's knowing how to do the perfect thing at the perfect time.

Sound like a high bar of excellence? It is.

But great favor awaits those leaders who persistently pursue thoughtfulness toward others.

In the scriptures, Saint Paul sent Timothy, his spiritual son, to the Church at Philippi saying, *"I have no one else like him, who will show genuine concern for your welfare."* (Phil. 2:20)

Timothy changed the world.

There are two kinds of attitudes leaders can attain:

---

1) Situational Thoughtfulness—those who give themselves only if they receive an advantage for doing so.

2) Perennial Thoughtfulness—those who give themselves (time, money, energy, effort) because it's the right way to live.

Situational Thoughtfulness

Situational leaders can move up the ladder of success and make more money. They figure out who is important for their personal advancements. Situational leaders then focus time and energy on being situationally thoughtful to those who can help them with their goals. The minute you, as a leader, decide to be thoughtful to one person instead of another because of what that person can do for you--you have become manipulative.

Situational leaders run into problems down the road. Emotionally, spiritually, and mentally a situational leader realizes they are only playing a game with others to be rewarded. Such manipulation taxes the mind, heart, and spirit. Situational leaders may advance and achieve their earthly career goals. But situational thoughtfulness is a recipe for a hollow life--losing yourself, your soul, and short-changing who you want to become in life.

Perennial Thoughtfulness

Perennial means long-lasting or long standing. **The leader who has decided to be a long-standing thoughtful person is a leader who will treat each person thoughtfully regardless of rank, station, or status.** Perennially Thoughtful leaders spend their lives being thoughtful to janitors & CEO's, poor folks & rich folks, commoners & well-connected individuals.

Why expend the extra energy, time, and effort? It's the right way to live!

The greatest example of thoughtful giving is found nowhere else but Christ. Of Christ Jesus, it was said, *"[He] did not consider equality with God something to be used to his own advantage; rather, he made himself nothing by taking the very nature of a servant, being made in human likeness."* (Phil. 2:6-7)

Three things we should note about Perennially Thoughtful Leaders:

> 1) They change the lives of people.
>
> 2) They change bad situations into good ones.
>
> 3) They become influential.

Thoughtful leaders are givers, not takers. They are grateful, not bitter. Thoughtful people sacrifice instead of preserve their energy and time.

Perennial Thoughtfulness is a way of life. It's how to become the leader you are called to be.

Question #1:

On a scale from 1 to 10, how well do you employ the Power of Thoughtfulness each day?

1	2	3	4	5	6	7	8	9	10

As a leader, if you chose to be more thoughtful about your words and actions, what might be the effect on your career?

_____

_____

POWER OF FAVOR

Some leaders excel beyond other leaders because they have the Power of Favor.

Favor is receiving preferential treatment; to be called out or chosen; treated differently; to receive advancement or extraordinary benefit.

Consider two leaders who execute a game plan equally well. Should they both have equal favor in the eyes of those who are watching their performance?

The short answer is: **Two leaders will rarely have equal favor even if they both achieve their goals at high levels.**

It's not just executing the game plan that matters. It's how others have been impacted by your leadership that determines the favor that leader receives.

How does a leader acquire the Power of Favor? Ask these two questions:

> 1) To what extent are you trusted?
> 2) How well do you build others?

Trust Factor

- Do people have to watch over you to get you to produce exceptional results?
- Are you having to be constantly reminded about following through or completing your tasks?
- How much energy do you cost others around you in achieving superior results?
- Do other people around you produce better results because of your impact in their lives?

Remember that if a leader delivers amazing results but at a high emotional cost to others, that leader will not win favor.

Favor is receiving advancement or extraordinary benefit.

Building Others Factor

- Are other people better off because of your presence after each encounter?
- Are you inspiring others around you to become better?
- Do others look to you for leadership?
- Does your leadership drive better performance from those around you?

Leaders who create energy for others instead of drain the energy of others become favored. Leaders who drain the energy of others will not receive favor. **Leaders who uplift others while at the same time achieving stellar results are ones who earn favor.** Leaders who do not achieve superior results while uplifting others may or may not receive favor.

The Power of Favor is reserved for special leaders who are builders of others and are achievers of superior performance.

In II Samuel, King Saul in 1050 BC watched his leadership evaporate in front of the nation of Israel. He proved untrustworthy. He was not a builder of others. Samuel, the beloved prophet of Israel, confronted King Saul and stripped this king of his moral authority. The Power of Favor landed on a harp-playing kid named David who was faithful to what was true in life. The teenage David courageously slew 7-foot tall Goliath, led and won multiple military battles and honored King Saul despite Saul's failures as a leader. Seventeen years of living by a code of trust and building others finally positioned David to be King of Israel.

When leaders can use their human capital to build others, make them better, and deliver better results, the Power of Favor comes upon them.

It's not enough to succeed. There are plenty of flawed leaders who succeed at achieving financial results. But the Power of Favor comes upon those leaders who prepare others to be wildly successful.

Without the Power of Favor, a leader cannot move higher. Be the leader today who receives the Power of Favor with others so your leadership becomes more influential and significant.

Question #1:

On a scale from 1 to 10, how much is the Power of Favor reflected in your life?

1	2	3	4	5	6	7	8	9	10

In your opinion, why do some leaders gain greater favor than other leaders?

_____

_____

POWER OF BEAUTY

Beauty has its own language. It speaks to the heart without ever saying a word. **Beauty has the power to arrest the soul. Beauty orders things in their right place.** There is no argument with beauty. You see it. You understand it. It brings tranquility to chaos. The Power of Beauty approaches perfection in a way nothing else can.

Beauty is its own perfection. It's unique, rare, and pleasing. It speaks to the heart and the mind simultaneously. Neither the heart nor the mind can resist affirming the Power of Beauty and when it is seen.

So, what exactly is the Power of Beauty and what does a good leader do with the Power of Beauty?

Beauty is perfection because it speaks of wholeness, fullness, and rarity of excellence. Beauty is the standard. It creates the order of how things are supposed to be.

For a good leader, he recognizes that the Power of Beauty comes in all forms and in all paths of life. The mess of papers all over a manager's desk is ugly. It lacks order. There is confusion. But once the papers are properly filed, beauty arises. Order is established. Whether it's a sunset, a geometrical equation, amazing athletic ability, masterful music, extraordinary intelligence, special kindness, or remarkable achievements, beauty abounds all around us.

Beauty does two things:

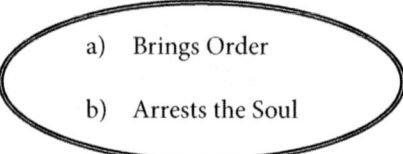

Beauty Brings Order

There is beauty in order. There is order in beauty. Good leaders are excellent in creating order from disorder or chaos. Dysfunction, failure, pain, and dissatisfaction are transformed when a good leader creates order.

When a leader creates order it's in one of two ways:

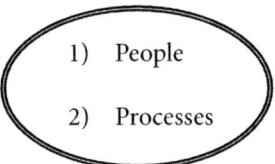

People

People around you constantly have problems. Problems are often born of confusion. Confusion is ugly and destructive. A good leader helps people solve their problems by creating necessary order for beauty to come alive in their lives.

Processes

Processes can be dysfunctional or inefficient. Inefficient and dysfunctional processes are frustrating and demoralizing. When a good leader creates better order in systems so they function at the highest capacity, this is a type of beauty. It's beauty because it approaches perfection.

Beauty Arrests the Soul

The soul is made up of mind, will, and emotion. The mind and emotions tend to move a million miles an hour without stopping during the day. It's exhausting. Many times, it's unproductive. Beauty stops the madness.

The mind and emotions, when presented with beauty, are brought to tranquility. Time stops. Beauty brings refreshment to the soul, imagination to the mind, and inspiration to the spirit.

The soul lives with a desperate need to be captured or arrested by beauty. From the marvels of engineering to nature to mathematical symmetries to remarkable athletic feats—the good leader engages people with the highest of virtues.

The Power of Beauty in Jesus' life is his ability to arrest the soul and bring order to life. Jesus said:

"Come to me, all you who are weary and burdened, and I will give you rest...if anyone is thirsty let him come to me and drink." (Matt. 11:28-30)

"I am the light of the world. Whoever follows me will never walk in darkness, but will have the light of life." (John 8:12)

"I have come that they may have life, and have it to the full." (John 10:10)

There is such simplistic beauty in these words.

The good leader uses the Power of Beauty to touch the soul. Through the soul, a good leader inspires others to become who they are supposed to be.

Question #1:

On a scale from 1 to 10, how much are your inspired by the Power of Beauty to perfect what you do?

1	2	3	4	5	6	7	8	9	10

Describe how the Power of Beauty inspires you to perfect what you do as a leader:

_____

_____

POWER OF ELIMINATION

Learn to eliminate what doesn't belong. Learn to eliminate what isn't a priority. Select the single most important thing to you in life and eliminate those hindrances that keep you from focusing on that one thing. What if you eliminated everything that wasted your time and energy?

Elimination is simplifying. The leader who takes away a distracting project or an idea allows greater focus on what's left to do. Leaders who don't know what to eliminate from their schedules or their lives are likely to bring:

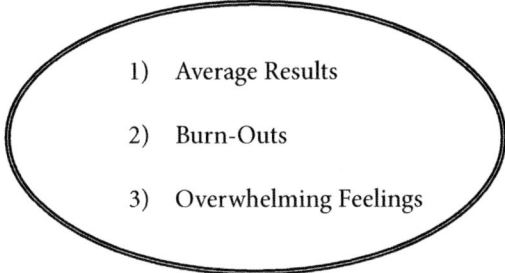

The power of elimination produces clarity, focus, and maximum capacity.

Clarity

How clear is my vision?

One of the reasons leaders can have a difficult time delivering superior results is because there is a lack of clarity about what or how things should be completed. A leader can have the energy. A leader can have the desire. **But when leaders fail to eliminate the distractions that get in the way of a clear vision, the vision becomes distorted or unreachable.** Too many competing interests for time means not enough energy for the one thing that matters. Only clarity delivers a chance to succeed at the highest level.

Focus

How much extra time and energy can I apply toward my vision?

Focus is the purposefully directed intelligent energy toward a vision.

When a leader eliminates competing interests for time and energy, that leader can focus his mental, spiritual, and emotional energies toward the important vision. **When you, as a leader, directly focus on a specific goal or vision with uninterrupted intelligent energy, you become a powerful force. Competing interests are the enemy of focus.** To focus means to see it all the way through. But you, as a leader, will have trouble seeing your goals and vision met all the way through if there is constant draining of energy and focus toward other matters in your life. **Great achievements are born from consistent focus.**

Capacity

The greater reserve capacity of energy and time you have, as a leader, the greater you can tackle and overcome the challenges in the way of meeting your goals. **Eliminating competing interests creates capacity.** You, as a leader, should be constantly asking what needs to be eliminated to expand capacity and achieve prioritized goals.

One leader's capacity can be greater than another leader's capacity because the first leader eliminates distractions and over-booked schedules. The first leader says "no" to good things in life that don't rise to being the most important things. The second leader doesn't say "no" to distractions as effectively. **Creating capacity is about having extra energy and time to focus on achieving the goals that you, as a leader, are serious about.**

Consider what to eliminate from your schedule. What is getting in the way of you achieving the goals you want to achieve? **By eliminating less important tasks, you create greater clarity, focus, and capacity for your vision.**

Question #1:

On a scale from 1 to 10, how effective are you at using the Power of Elimination to eliminate those things in the way of your priorities?

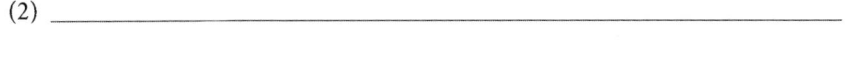

List two specific things you can eliminate that get in the way of your priorities regularly:

(1) _____

_____

(2) _____

_____

POWER OF OPTIMISM

Key Word: Optimism – "the tendency to be hopeful and the feeling that in the future good things are more likely to happen than bad things."

This quality, more than any other, can get others to perform and be better at what they do. Optimism is good for the soul. It says that if I do what I am supposed to do today, I will achieve today and be even better tomorrow. An optimistic leader does not allow the failure of other people to change the way that leader sees life, work, and the future.

Optimism does not allow you to wear down quickly. An optimistic leader creates an oasis environment where others feel like they can flourish, and enjoy growing as people.

Life throws difficult emotional, mental and, physical twists everyone's way. No one escapes this reality. Optimistic leaders, however, do one thing better than most other leaders. They are able to spark an energy, enthusiasm, and a belief in other people so that what they are doing today is important for who they are becoming.

How do we become optimistic, as a general rule?

---

1) Get up in the morning early with intention to succeed.

2) Purposefully smile; see how you feel---science shows that if you smile you release hormones that actually contribute to well-being.

3) Believe in people that are in your sphere of influence—really believe in them.

4) See the people you work with as "they will be one day" instead of as they are today.

5) Keep your mind on the ultimate prize that you are becoming uniquely gifted as a leader as you grow.

Here's the good news! If you are an aspiring leader, you can train your mind to become the optimistic leader that you appreciate. Optimism takes work minute by minute. But optimism creates extra energy and focus that most of the time average leaders don't tap into.

Don't just meet the goals and think you did what you were supposed to. Harness the power of optimism and change the way people around you live, think, and act.

Optimism is a choice to live the better way!

Question #1:

On a scale from 1 to 10, how much do you radiate optimism in the presence of others?

| 1 | 2 | 3 | 4 | 5 | 6 | 7 | 8 | 9 | 10 |

What one specific habit can you improve to be more optimistic in your life?

_____

_____

POWER OF PRIORITIES

Effective leaders find a way to organize themselves around priorities that matter. One of the great disappointments in leadership is often a leader's inability to organize around priorities. Ineffective leaders either don't write the goals down, or they simply don't know what they should prioritize. Either case will deliver poor results for themselves and their teammates.

Effective leaders are adamant about **organizing around priority items**. They write these priorities down. These leaders insist that the entire team organize around priorities and work toward meeting these highly-valued goals. These leaders know that not every task, thought, or action item is equally valuable. Effective leaders are always measuring the amount of time it will take to complete what is important. These leaders are constantly measuring work being completed on the timetable of a schedule.

All effective leaders operate well within established time constraints. They realize the absolute necessity of knowing how to accomplish more with less.

There are 3 questions every effective leader asks when **prioritizing activities and personnel**:

1) W - What has to be completed?
2) W - When does it have to be completed?
3) W - Who is going to complete it?

If you can reflect on these three questions for every task that has to be completed, then you will improve your leadership effectiveness.

3W Paradigm

> W - Average Leaders -- Know what has to be completed.
>
> WW - Good leaders -- Know what has to be completed and when the task has to be complete.
>
> WWW - Most effective leaders -- Know what, when and who is best suited to complete the task.

By critically thinking through the 3-W Paradigm, this leader consistently wins by organizing around priorities.

You know great leaders by the results they produce. But results are not magic. They are well-thought out game plans that **organize people and schedules around priorities.**

Question #1:

On a scale from 1 to 10, how well do you organize around the most important priorities?

1	2	3	4	5	6	7	8	9	10

If you could change one habit that would help you execute your priorities better, describe what that change would be:

_____

_____

POWER OF TRANSPARENCY

You can tell how healthy a leader is or how healthy a culture is by how they handle mistakes.

Errors and mistakes are made all the time. The question is how do we handle it? There are 3 ways to respond:

> 1) Hide the mistake out of fear.
>
> 2) Hide the mistake out of intellectual superiority (too good to admit it).
>
> 3) Admit the mistake because I have chosen to grow through the struggles.

Two smart doctors with egos in a real-time surgery room can clash with their opinions. Even if the lead doctor recognizes he is wrong, he may risk the patient to avoid being humbled by the other doctor in the room. Sound crazy? It happens. Both of them employ a term called "Cognitive Dissonance" to intellectually defend their positions regardless of who is actually right or wrong!

You learn you are wrong. Instead of being humble and learning to grow through it, you fight the truth and run the opposite direction of transparency.

President Richard Nixon in 1974 resigned the presidency. Why? When he found out that his team had broken into opposing political party's headquarters to steal secret information, President Nixon covered it up. If he had come clean when he learned of what his team had done, resigning the office to avoid impeachment would have been highly unlikely. Forever, he will be remembered as a cover-up artist who lacked transparency.

Nearly every sibling learns early in life how to verbally argue their brothers and sisters. How often does the argument get to the point where it doesn't matter whether you are wrong anymore? You won't admit it. You know you are wrong. Instead, you then employ brilliant intelligence and verbal strategies to avoid being caught or being wrong in front of that other person. You are caught defending what you know is wrong.

What can you learn about smart executives who fail? It's usually not failure in a strategy or goal that delivers failed results to an executive. It's staying with a strategy too long and not admitting the marketplace has changed, or his calculations were wrong in the beginning, or he employed the wrong personnel for the mission. Instead, he rationalizes the matter. He gets paid so much money that he believes he has to be right and can't be wrong. He sticks to the plan out of a superiority complex even though deep down he knows he should take corrective action.

When you combine Intelligence and Ego, you are a danger to progress, growth, and to the success of other people around you.

Incidentally, the longer and higher a leader rises in their profession, the greater likelihood that this leader may implement denial strategies about being wrong about nearly anything. That is, unless that leader intentionally commits to the principle of Transparency. Transparency will allow you to never become a "know it all" and does allow you to walk more humbly about your decision-making.

Admit the error or mistake so that you can grow through it and create greater tacit knowledge. Don't let intelligence and ego combine to stand in the way of your progress and your destiny.

A good leader understands that mistakes are inevitable. Most mistakes are correctable. Be prepared and willing to admit error quickly and without reservation so that your energy can be focused on building a better future.

Question #1:

On a scale from 1 to 10, how quickly do you, as a leader, admit your mistakes?

1	2	3	4	5	6	7	8	9	10

What is it most difficult for you, as a leader, to be transparent with those with whom you work?

_____

_____

POWER OF GOAL SETTING

Goal-setting, when done correctly, is an exercise in imagining who you can be. The highest form of goal-setting is combining your inspiration, your imagination, and your initiative to become who you want to be.

Imagination by itself cannot be converted to effective goal-setting until there is:

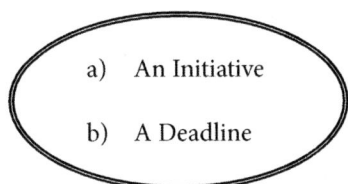

Lots of leaders dream and imagine, but they fail to accomplish much. Why? Because most significant accomplishments that last are born from the labor of imagination. **Imagination is the fuel to your fire.** It's the energy for initiative. Without engaging your imagination, you are a robot going through the motions of life. You can achieve certain goals. But you won't become who you want to be fully until you carve out time regularly to imagine and marvel at the idea of imagination.

Stop and imagine for a moment. Just imagine. Feel the torrent of possibilities, excitement, and energy that overwhelms you. **When you take time to practice imagining who you want to be, your destiny comes alive.**

"Magic" is a word closely associated with imagine. Magic completely enthralls, enraptures, and takes over the mind with an idea.

As the University Program Coordinator in college at UNT, I once brought a magician into the Rock Bottom Lounge. He levitated a young lady lying flat on the bar room table by about two feet. I experienced a remarkable rush of "awe" that came over me. It was surely a cheap parlor trick. I get it. But this moment opened me to possibilities of what could be!

Imagination, each day, takes you to a place that your current life cannot. It takes you to who you are becoming—if you will let it.

All of this talk about imagination—why? You cannot set effective goals that mean anything until you imagine!

Without investing in your imagination, you will have little inspiration to change who you are today. Goals will be worthless. Only when you are inspired by your imagination can you become an effective goal-setting leader.

Do you want to lead well? **Learn to imagine first. That is fuel to inspiration. Once inspired, you can initiate the kind of goal-setting that will drive you to your destiny.**

The goals will be clear. The goals will have deadlines. You will have the inspiration and energy to accomplish your mission in life.

Question #1:

On a scale from 1 to 10, how effectively do you use your imagination to attain important goals?

1	2	3	4	5	6	7	8	9	10

What two specific concrete-steps can you take as a leader to improve goal-setting in your life?

(1) _____

_____

(2) _____

_____

POWER OF INSPIRATION

Is information or inspiration needed more in lives of leaders today?

More times than not, leaders who are inspired find ways to achieve their goals. Leaders who have acquired lots of information have exactly that—lots of information. They are smarter. They are capable. They can achieve. But leaders who learn more aren't necessarily the leaders who are going to change the world.

Knowledge alone is not the answer to effective leadership. Knowledge must be applied toward a leader's vision that is inspired. Inspiration is the "**action or power of moving the intellect or emotions.**"

Inspiration does for a leader what nothing else can. It **conquers fear**. It fights through obstacles, problems, and challenges that are huge. Perseverance and grit, when combined with inspiration, creates execution that is nearly unstoppable. Inspiration aligns with unity the heart and the mind to march forward toward a goal.

The man who is inspired by his destiny will train at the gym more consistently, eat healthier, and work toward building personal character. This leader will be happier and more teachable. This leader will tend to be more prepared.

Inspiration will impel a leader to become who he or she needs to become to achieve the goal. Too much information can overload the brain and paralyze a leader's ability to act. Too much inspiration—well, there may not be such a thing? Inspiration is the fuel necessary to initiate action and work toward a vision. Information allows you to be smart about tackling problems. Inspiration will allow you to actually stop talking about tackling the problem and get into middle of a problem to solve it.

With inspiration, a leader finds his or her place in the world. That leader finds who they are, what they want to become, and how they want to be remembered.

Information is valuable. Inspiration is indispensable. An inspired leader will have all of his or her intellect and emotions moved toward achieving vision of their life. Whatever information an inspired leader is lacking, this leader will find it to achieve the goal.

A final question remains: How well does your leadership inspire others to be their best and for you to be your best?

Question #1:

On a scale from 1 to 10, how inspired are you as a leader?

| 1 | 2 | 3 | 4 | 5 | 6 | 7 | 8 | 9 | 10 |

What one specific action step can you take to be more inspiring to others?

_____

_____

POWER OF HABITS

Key Word: Habit – "a particular act or way of acting that you tend to do regularly."

Aristotle once said, "We are what we repeatedly do. Excellence, then, is not an act, but a habit."

It is estimated that you make about 35,000 choices per day with respect to all types of activities. These choices are often driven by habits that we have created, some good and some poor. No person can ever free themselves from having habits. Habits are here to stay. If you know this as a leader, then you can use the power of habits to create a better you!

What if over 60 years you know that you had 3,000 choices per day to make? That would be just over 6 million choices you make in a lifetime. Most of these choices are made by habits.

Habits can be replaced; not eliminated. **Effective leaders are better at replacing bad habits with good habits** than most other people. Effective leaders become more influential, have more responsibility, and succeed at a higher level.

Study any leader that has been effective and you will see how they replaced bad habits with good habits consistently and successfully.

The question remains--how do we change our bad habits into good habits? Human beings are complex creatures. Charles Duhigg, in his book called, "The Power of Habit" suggests that there are 3 parts to habits:

1) Trigger	2) Routine	3) Reward
Stress	Smoke	Calmness

The trigger, in this case, is stress. The bad habit is smoking that produces the reward which is calmness.

Duhigg argues that stress can remain the trigger, however, **changing the routine** of the stress by creating a different routine is the answer to achieving the reward-- calmness.

A powerful tool for this person is to write down how he feels in a journal every time he begins feeling stressed instead of lighting up the cigarette for seven days. By doing this, a person becomes self-aware of their routine. Most of us employ our routines as a matter of habit without thinking about it. We have programmed our minds and bodies into responding to triggers, routines, and rewards!

The goal is to choose a certain behavior ahead of time once we are aware of the trigger that causes the routine to effortlessly kick in. It's the routine that should change, which delivers the same reward.

The struggling man says, "I feel stress coming on right now."

What is his next step? He has already decided to act differently. He will choose differently when the stress trigger pops up. So, he steps out of the office, walks around the block, and eats a red apple while walking.

Does this work? Research is still being compiled.

But what we do know is that people who wish to lose 100 pounds, quit smoking, get their PHD, become millionaires, or become effective leaders have done so by replacing natural habits or bad habits with deliberate and intentionally good habits. We will always have triggers in our lives. We will always have routines and rewards. The question for all aspiring leaders is how much they are willing to change their routines causing the triggers in their life in order to deliver greater rewards.

Life is short. Create good habits today!

"Habits are routines. The difference between an amateur and a professional is in their habits. An amateur has amateur habits. A professional has professional habits. We can never free ourselves from habit. But we can replace bad habits with good ones." - Steven Pressfield

Question #1:

On a scale from 1 to 10, how effective are you at replacing bad habits with good habits?

| 1 | 2 | 3 | 4 | 5 | 6 | 7 | 8 | 9 | 10 |

Reflect on a bad habit that you want to improve. Describe the strategy, as a leader, you can employ to turn the bad habit into a good one:

_____

_____

POWER OF LOVE

The greatest description of love given in Scripture is as follows in I Corinthians 13—

> "Love is patient, love is kind. It does not envy, it does not boast, it is not proud. It does not dishonor others, it is not self-seeking, it is not easily angered, it keeps no record of wrongs. Love does not delight in evil but rejoices with the truth. It always protects, always trusts, always hopes, always perseveres. Love never fails. But where there are prophecies, they will cease; where there are tongues, they will be stilled; where there is knowledge, it will pass away. And now these three remain: faith, hope and love. But the greatest of these is love."

The bible has 4 different words it uses in the ancient Greek for love:

---

1) Eros: Erotic love; romance and passion.

2) Filia: Brotherly love; between people who share common values & interests.

3) Storge: Parent-child relationship; most natural of all loves; born of familiarity.

4) Agape: Unconditional love; serves regardless of changing circumstances.

All of these types of love are part of the human capacity and experience. But as C.S. Lewis wrote in his book called "The Four Loves", the first 3 loves above should subordinate themselves to Agape love, the greatest love of all.

When a leader transcends the many petty squabbles and struggles of daily existence, and instead chooses to live from Agape Love, that leader will be a people developer among those around him. Do I love those around me for what they can do for me? Or do I love them "Agape" style?

Leaders who grow to maturity develop an "Agape" Love for others. No matter what that person does to me, I will "Agape" love this person. When Jesus walked the hills of Galilee, there wasn't a leper, prostitute, outcast, blind man, or diseased person who wasn't transformed by the "Agape" Love that flowed from Him. Eleven out of the twelve disciples walked three years with Jesus. They were so moved by the power of "Agape" Love that they gave up their lives as martyrs for the cause of Christ. When Jesus was nailed to the cross in agony and pain, some of his final words were, *"Father, forgive them—for they know not what they are doing."* (Luke 23:34)

"Agape" Love is the rarest of the four loves. "Agape" Love does not abandon others. It loves to the point of death.

"Agape" Love is the most life-changing and powerful from which a leader can be personally transformed while helping others transform their identity, vision, and destiny.

Just in case there is a lingering thought that "Agape" Love will create more material wealth or instantly secure better career opportunity—banish that thought immediately. "Agape" Love is not a genie bottle that can be rubbed for three wishes at your command to shape your future.

The "Agape" Leader will toil serving others often unnoticed. Time, energy, and money will be spent on others, of which some will be appreciated and others will simply disappear. But the leader who creates "Agape" habits minute by minute each day, will have invested the human capital in others that will be his crown of greatness.

Of this leader, it will be said, *"Well done, my good and faithful servant."* (Matt. 25:23)

Question #1:

On a scale from 1 to 10, how much does your life reflect "Agape" Love for those with whom you work each day?

| 1 | 2 | 3 | 4 | 5 | 6 | 7 | 8 | 9 | 10 |

How does an individual come to a place in their life to unconditionally love others as a matter of practice?

_____

_____

POWER OF THE PROBLEM SOLVER

Effective leaders solve problems. Average leaders put problems on the backs of others or deem them as currently unimportant. You can see these leadership habits develop at an early age. How many kids do you remember that hated math at an early age. Why? Math, like the multiplication tables, algebra, and geometry demands significant mental energy. That child is actually tearing down the brain muscle. It's just like going to the gym and working out. It hurts!

But this discipline to train the mind and accustom this muscle to grow and develop is the very habit that separates effective leaders from average leaders.

Effective leaders are simply willing to **put out the energy necessary that drains the brain.** They willingly choose to solve problems that other leaders will wait for others to solve. Average leaders might say, "I don't know how to," "I've never done that," "If I only had better," or "That's really not my area of expertise."

This is not the language of effective leaders. An effective leader begins training their own mind by rewriting their own language script: "Let me see how we can resolve this. Maybe there is a better way? Who can I get to help me learn more about this issue?"

Any leader can return phone calls, answer fifteen emails, and smile. But these rote tasks will not differentiate a leader as effective. Rote and routine tasks feel good to complete because it feels like work is being completed. But the work that separates great leaders from good ones is the ability to critically think and organize viable solutions for the team.

The reason problems are problems in life is because of the large amount of energy and intelligence it takes to solve that problem. It's easy for a leader who has many things on her plate to allow the problem to sit there.

The average leader asks, "Why should I solve this problem when no one else has taken the time to solve it already? Once someone solves this problem, I will follow the marching orders and use the solution that gets the best results once someone else uses their brainpower to solve the problem."

The effective leader says: "Stop everything. Does this make sense? If it doesn't, how do I solve this problem?"

If the problem is crime, poor technology, poor financial results, poor relationships, poor evaluations or sub-par performance of any other kind, the effective leaders uses brain power to:

---

1) Understand what the problem is.

2) Ask why the problem is occurring.

3) Formulate possible solutions to solve the problem.

4) Evaluate the chosen solution to see if it works well enough.

The Problems Solving Leader is not necessarily smarter. He just want to be better.

That leader has already decided that their mind will face exhaustion on some days trying to solve problems. The Problem-Solving Leader has decided, like the one doing mathematics, that he will endure the hurt that comes from using the mind with greater intensity. When leaders have already chosen this as a lifestyle, they become effective leaders and receive more opportunities to achieve higher goals.

Question #1:

On a scale from 1 to 10, how effectively do you solve problems as a leader?

| 1 | 2 | 3 | 4 | 5 | 6 | 7 | 8 | 9 | 10 |

What one strategy can you implement to improve becoming a better Problem Solver than you are today?

_____

_____

POWER OF A CEO MINDSET

Are You a Salesman or CEO?

Two kinds of productive leaders exist. It's the Salesman and the CEO.

We cannot live without salesmanship. Everybody has some salesmanship in their being whether it's selling a service or a product. In fact, an old adage says, "Sales Solves All Problems." An organization that is selling, growing, and developing is one that makes people in the organization feel like they are on a winning team and going somewhere. This is good.

Peering a little deeper into the differences between a salesman mindset and one of a CEO, we might ask ourselves, do I act more like a salesman or CEO?

There is a term called the "Salesman's Curse" versus having a CEO Mindset. Leaders often fall into one of these two categories:

Salesman Mindset

- Hunts for excellent performance; highly driven to achieve the goal.
- Achieves excellent performance, receives their award then checks out emotionally until forced to perform again; which could be weeks or months.
- This sends conflicting leadership messages to the rest of the organization.

CEO Mindset

- Continuously seeks high performance.
- Steadily works toward winning and achieving goals.

> - Doesn't let a victory derail the consistent persistence of getting better.
> - Presses in after a victory and helps others grow in their confidence and leadership abilities.

What is the salesman's curse? It's slowing down after achieving a victory. It's hitting the goals for the month, then turning around and taking it easy, thinking that everybody should be happy. It's receiving the bonus money for achieving your goals and then emotionally checking out of work. A salesman's mindset may win big bonuses or have good months. But a salesman's mindset will not build up organizations or people to be leaders. For those people are simply salesmen, this work alright. But for those leaders who are moving to higher levels in their leadership, the salesman's curse actually hurts the people around the salesman and limits the ability of the organization to become better!

The CEO mindset has a long-term view of his leadership and the organization. When he wins a big bonus, he stays focused on the "bigger picture" making himself and others better in the organization. He understands people depend on him to deliver consistently improving results. The CEO Mindset has a higher "emotional intelligence" and chooses to care about others consistently in a way that builds them up.

We need the salesman in our organization. Even executives need to have some salesman qualities in them. But when you succeed, carefully ask yourself a few questions. Do I take a mental vacation away from everyone? Or do I think like a CEO using this recent victory to create momentum for the entire team helping others meet their goals?

Question #1:

On a scale from 1 to 10, how well do you focus on achieving more after a big reward or victory?

1	2	3	4	5	6	7	8	9	10

As a leader, what one concrete-step can you take to focus after a big victory?

_____

_____

POWER OF A GOOD GREAT LEADER

Is Your Leadership Good, Great, or Both?

Good leaders accomplish their goals by building others up along the way as a primary part of their mission statement.

Great leaders accomplish their goals at nearly any cost even if it means others are expendable in the process of becoming great.

There is, however, a unique leader in life who is a Good Great Leader. **The Good Great Leader finds a way to accomplish his goal (that's being great) while honoring others and building them up along the way (that's being good).**

Is it possible to be great and not be good? Yes. Alexander "The Great" conquered more territory than any military leader in history. But there was nothing remarkably good about this man. Napoleon conquered territory, but few would argue he was a good leader, though his military tactics and ability to shape the world classify him as a great leader.

Good is a moral quality that speaks to a leader's relational abilities to change someone's life for the better. The good leader does not suspend his moral quality of "goodness" to achieve a great objective. The great leader might do that. The good leader will never do that.

The good leader has decided that he will only be great when he can develop those around him so they become better through the goodness that he himself lives by. Where might this goodness be found to live by?

Saint Paul speaks of the highest and greatest test of Good Leadership in I Corinthians 13:4-7:

> *"Love is patient, love is kind. It does not envy, it does not boast, it is not proud. It does not dishonor others, it is not self-seeking, it is not easily angered, it keeps no*

record of wrongs. Love does not delight in evil but rejoices with the truth. It always protects, always trusts, always hopes, always perseveres."

Now replace the word love with your name and read the above passage again.

The impact is incredible. Do you really want to be a good leader? These are the moral attributes every good leader strives for. How well do you do replacing the word love with your name?

In business, it's called human capital. In relational terms, it's called love.

The good leader's highest and greatest call in life is to make the lives of others better so those around him can help that leader achieve the objectives set before him. When others around you truly believe that you are for them fully, you will be on your way to becoming a Good Great Leader.

Question #1:

On a scale from 1 to 10, how much of a Good Great Leader are you striving to be?

1	2	3	4	5	6	7	8	9	10

As a leader, what one action-step can you implement to significantly improve your ability to be a Good Great Leader?

_____

_____

POWER OF SELF-REFLECTION

Who Am I?

When no one is looking: Who am I? How trustworthy am I to be the leader I am called to be?

Look in the mirror. **A true assessment of character is determined by what you do and how you think when you aren't on stage performing for others.** When you are alone with no direct supervision handling the daily routine, are you as sensitive to excellence as when others are watching—is what you do good? Is it bad?

When no one is looking, I am as focused on achieving my goals as when others are paying attention to me.

When no one is looking, I am as productive as when others are paying attention to my actions.

When no one is looking, I get away with little things that I wouldn't try to get away when others are paying attention.

When no one is looking, my personal issues and time on social media rises significantly higher.

As an aspiring leader, your character is what you have to rely on to become better. Your feelings will lead you astray because they are inconsistent, fickle, and will turn others away from you. Only good character promotes an aspiring leader from good to great.

Even when an aspiring leader who is a rising star in an organization delivers excellent results, they should assess for themselves how trustworthy they are as a leader by answering: Am I trustworthy when I am alone? If I was supervising my alone time as an honest, third-party assessor, would I be pleased with the findings?

Aspiring leaders who want to be great learn to discipline their minds and their efforts to be their best when others aren't looking. **Aspiring leaders understand that good character isn't turned on and off depending on who is watching.** That's the definition of bad character.

Will you be the best when no one is looking? Leaders aspiring to be great do exactly this.

Question #1:

On a scale from 1 to 10, how well do you use the Power of Self-Reflection to become a better leader?

| 1 | 2 | 3 | 4 | 5 | 6 | 7 | 8 | 9 | 10 |

Describe how self-reflection improves your ability to lead:

_____

_____

POWER OF PURPOSE

Who am I? Where am I going? Why am I here?

Philosophers, theologians, academic institutions, synagogues, and churches are places that seek to understand what is true and how we should live. Good leaders are grounded in striving to fulfill their purposes in life. The psalmist says, "Life is but a mist", here today and gone tomorrow. Unless we live with a more noble cause, a higher calling, then what good are the activities we pursue? In fact, no matter who the leader is— **without a higher purpose, our lives fall apart and eventually become uninspiring.**

Jesus told a parable. A hard-working capitalist who never cheated anybody had reaped a reward from the planting of his crops. It was a big reward. This man chose to build bigger barns with no thought to build others or serve a higher cause in life. More bumper crops arrived and filled the barns to overflowing. This man was gifted, talented, and very capable with his abilities.

Jesus gave the punch line to the story saying, *"But God said to him, 'You fool! This very night your life will be demanded from you. Then who will get what you have prepared for yourself?"* (Luke 12:20)

Jesus said it to another individual in slightly different language.

"What good will it be for someone to gain the whole world, yet forfeit their soul? Or what can anyone give in exchange for their soul?" (Matt. 16:26)

Good leaders appreciate advancement and creation of wealth because it is a reflection of their character and work ethic. Good leaders, however, don't leave people behind. They recognize their purpose is to serve others regardless of their own material achievements.

Good leaders purpose themselves to bring those around them along with them on the journey. Good leaders honor others as God has honored them.

The highest and **greatest of any purpose is "to know God"** and to know Him well. This is, after all, the place where the infinite supply of love, faith, hope, renewal, joy, and purpose is at your disposal if a leader chooses to tap into it each day. It is said that good leaders can be renewed to be their best as they fulfill their purpose!

All good things are grounded in this highest call that every leader is to answer. The psalmist says, *"You are my Lord; apart from you I have no good thing."* Psalm 16:2

Today, be implored to make your highest calling to serve and love with "all your heart, mind, and soul."

An expert in the law, tested Jesus with this question, *"'Teacher, which is the greatest commandment in the Law?'*

Jesus replied, 'Love the Lord your God with all your heart and with all your soul and with all your mind and with all your strength;' [and,] 'Love your neighbor as yourself.'" (Matt. 22:35-39)

Good leaders learn to be extreme in following their purpose and not being distracted by selfish motives. **Good leaders invest their human capital by choosing to serve others, build others up,** and live in such a way as to honor their purpose and high calling in life so that it may be well with their soul.

Question #1:

On a scale from 1 to 10, how much does the Power of Purpose in life drive your leadership?

1	2	3	4	5	6	7	8	9	10

Describe how you are using the Power of Purpose in your life to achieve your goals:

_____

_____

POWER OF THE PROVERB

Proverbs were here long before you. They will be here long after you're gone. But there is wisdom in paying attention to Proverbs. **They give a good leader a focal point for living a better life.**

As a leader, you will make many difficult decisions throughout the course of your life. Leaders can make poor decisions, more times than not, because they lack a moral compass of right thinking.

Applying truisms from the Book of Proverbs across the spectrum of life **can help a good leader maintain a moral compass** that avoids destructive relationships and bad decision-making.

Charting the course of life on good, fixed, unchangeable ideas is what Proverbs helps us do. It focuses our hearts and minds before we act.

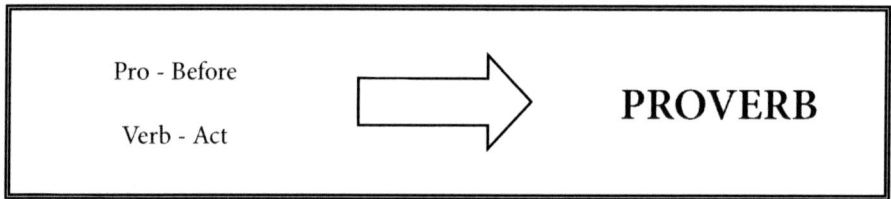

Before acting: Good Leaders think and reflect on what is true.

Proverbs reflects on what is just, right, and fair. They seek not just knowledge, but wisdom in how to apply knowledge.

Consider the following proverb:

"A gentle answer turns away wrath, but a harsh word stirs up anger." (Prov. 15:1)

A small verse put together over 3,000 years ago, that has power to capture your focus. Think about what your mind is doing right now reading this proverb. You are saying, "Yes, that really is true!"

You slowly replay the experiences of your own life. You recall those moments when you used wisdom to respond to another person instead of reacting impetuously. Do you remember the results?

"Reckless words pierce like a sword, but the tongue of the wise brings healing." (Prov. 12:10)

When Solomon wrote this proverb 3,000 years ago, who would have thought this timeless principle about reckless words would have so much meaning to us today? Does my tongue practice bringing healing or hurt to others?

"Diligent hands will rule, but laziness ends in slave labor." (Prov. 12:24)

Your leadership is always reflected by your example. Am I diligent or is it easy for me to be lazy? Also, what does it mean that laziness ends in slave labor?

"A cheerful look brings joy to the heart, and good news gives health to the bones." (Prov. 15:30)

What a way to live, right? A momentary focus on this little golden nugget can change the course of the day.

A proverb gives us the power to focus and think right before you act. The more we spend time reading through the Book of Proverbs in little bits at a time, the greater ability we will have to be the leader we want to be.

Good Leadership consistently applies the power of focus by investing in a good moral compass to guide us through life. The timeless principles laid out in bite-size nuggets prepare our hearts and minds to think and act well in each situation.

Question #1:

On a scale from 1 to 10, how well do you take time to implement nuggets of wisdom that you come across?

1	2	3	4	5	6	7	8	9	10

As a leader, what method could you use to improve how you gather wisdom?

_____

_____

POWER OF PERFORMANCE

The Power of Performance is about how far an aspiring leader can go to become who they are supposed to be. Performance is how we measure the targeted objectives.

The Power of Performance will help an aspiring leader grow to the next level in 2 specific ways:

Develop Trust

Trust is earned. Trust is nearly always built upon the back of superior performance. An aspiring leader who does not achieve the objectives for an organization loses the trust of others and becomes less valuable.

In sports terms, an aspiring leader who achieves objectives at high level, is like winning the championship game, World Series, or Super Bowl. When an aspiring leader overcomes obstacles, and achieves lofty goals, he or she becomes one of the most trusted figures. To be trusted is to be elevated to higher levels in the leadership journey.

Create Opportunities

Opportunities are reserved for those who harness the Power of Performance. The aspiring leader is likely to receive additional opportunities to move higher when they prove their value through the Power of Performance.

Opportunity is an aspiring leader's best friend. About 10,000 new actors and actresses migrate to Hollywood each year. They ask for no guarantee. These aspiring movie actors fight, scratch, and scrape each day only looking for an opportunity to showcase their talent. Every day, middle level managers, supervisors, salesmen, etc., do the same thing looking for the opportunity that will recognize their talent. In the marketplace, an aspiring leader's ability to consistently deliver superior performance is the single greatest factor in getting that leader the next opportunity.

The Power of Performance separates average leaders from leaders who are superior. Average leaders cannot be trusted with further levels of opportunities. Nor can average leaders expect opportunities to rise to the next level. Superior performance, however, can generate enormous amounts of trust and opportunities.

Learn to harness the Power of Performance. It is this measure that will allow leadership to be trusted at higher levels and create opportunities previously not available.

Question #1:

On a scale from 1 to 10, how well has the Power of your Performance opened additional leadership opportunities for you?

1	2	3	4	5	6	7	8	9	10

As a leader, what specific action-steps can you take to improve your leadership performance?

_____

_____

POWER OF DECISION

Key Word: Decision - "something you choose; a choice."

Captain Hernan Cortez landed at Veracruz in 1519 from Spain. To the amazement of his fellow soldiers, Cortez burned all the ships. There was no going back. The team would have to determine the way forward in a new land.

Instead of wallowing in indecision or turning backwards, Good Leaders employ the Power of Decision to trigger 3 specific leadership qualities:

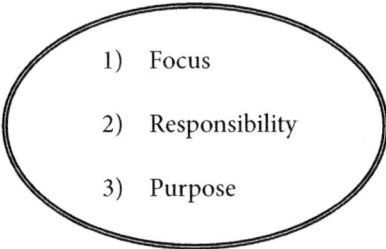

Focus

The Power of Decision empowers leaders to focus. Make the decision to move forward. When a Good Leader chooses the way forward with no escaping backwards, all energy—mental, emotional, physical, and spiritual can be aligned to achieve the goal. Complete alignment allows leaders to excel at the highest level.

Be aware that when a leader chooses to waffle, ruminate, worry, or appear indecisive for too long, those around that leader lose confidence and desire to serve the greater cause. No one wants to be led by a leader who lacks confidence to make a good decision or is unwilling to move forward.

The Power of Decision destroys all other options. It focuses you on what you must do with the one absolute decision that has been made.

Responsibility

Nothing makes a leader more responsible than making an absolute decision. That leader becomes responsible quickly to meet the goal.

Leaders who make soft decisions instead of absolute ones leave themselves escape valves in case difficulties arise. These leaders become demoralized more quickly. Their minds are not as tough. Their emotional resilience to bounce back is limited. Instead of focusing on getting the job done, a leader's focus scatters abroad thinking of whether there are other things they can be doing with their time or career.

The Power of Decision allows leaders to take full responsibility of the project, vision, or goal. The Power of Decision also allows Good Leaders to treat those around them with a greater empathy and desire to see others succeed.

Purpose

The Power of Decision produces purpose. People want purpose. Whatever else is happening in life, a firm decision to move forward means a Good Leader knows what must be accomplished. That leader will marshal all the forces of thought, wit, energy, and resources toward the purpose at hand. **Others will join a Good Leader who is driven by purpose.**

When leaders fail to rally around a decision forcefully, those leaders are unable to explain to other team members why they should give their full time and effort to that decision. The team may have remarkable talent. **But only when a Good Leader makes a firm decision can those around this leader rally around that decision with a purpose.**

Good Leaders employ the Power of Decision to create focus, responsibility, and purpose. This is how Good Leaders achieve goals. Lead well by deciding well. Focus on people and projects. **Take responsibility so all your creative intelligence and energy will truly be devoted to the cause.** The Power of Decision produces the necessary purpose to accomplish the goal.

Question #1:

On a scale from 1 to 10, how effectively do you employ the power of decision-making?

1	2	3	4	5	6	7	8	9	10

If you marginally improved the Power of Decision in your life, describe what effect that might have in your sphere of influence?

_____

_____

POWER OF PRESENTATION

Key Word: Presentation - "the act of giving or showing something."

Good Leaders are nearly always in presentation mode by "showing, describing, or explaining" vision and purpose.

How do you look? Sound? Act? Everything matters.

The Power of Presentation determines whether you break through to the next level in your vision and goals. There are lots of leaders who are virtuous and sincere. But these leaders hit a glass ceiling. They can only climb so far. Why?

It's the Image Effect—the way others perceive who you are.

How Do I Look?

- Is my outfit professional? Is it stained? Is it wrinkled?
- Is my hair groomed exceptionally well?
- Do I smile well?
- Do I look clean cut or am I a little sloppy?
- Do the shoes I wear stand out?
- Is my car clean? Is my house clean?
- Do I dress better than others?

The image you exhibit, whether true or not, delivers a perception to people about how you see yourself and how much you care about what you are doing. Is it possible to be a Good Leader and get good results and still be held back because of the "Image Effect?"

Answer: Yes. The "Image Effect" is so powerful that it can speak against a Good Leader.

How Do I Sound?

How do I sound to others? The words we communicate can "make or break" a Good Leader. **A Good Leader can spend months building relationships well with well-timed words of affirmation and team-building. But in two sentences, that same Good Leader can set herself back by using unwise words, gossip, or engage in destructive language.**

How you sound as a leader ranks highly in determining how well you are trusted and how far you go in your leadership.

- Do I talk too much? Too little?
- Do I talk at just the right time?
- Does what I say lift others up?
- Do I laugh enough?
- Does what I say add value to the conversation?
- Do I ask people lots of questions about their life?
- Do I talk about others (gossip)?
- Do I read enough, reflect enough, etc., to create meaningful dialogue?

The Power of Presentation means Good Leaders are self-aware and are learning about themselves continually. They want to know if others are turned off, offended, or indifferent by a Good Leader's words.

How Do I Act?

- Do I cut people off?
- Do I let people have their say?
- Do listen well?
- Do I exhibit human capital?
- Am I too busy to live now and care for each person in my presence?
- Do I look people in the eye and listen intently to them?
- Do I use my cell phone while others are trying to talk to me?
- Do I give my best to the job and others?

The better a Good Leader conducts himself in the presence of others, the greater the Power of Presentation will be for this leader.

The Power of Presentation can help a Good Leader achieve his destiny much more quickly than nearly anything else. The reasons are as follows:

1) Power of Presentation is all in the Good Leader's Control.
2) Power of Presentation can be improved every day to reach the goal.
3) Power of Presentation compels others to become better also.

What are you known for as a leader? Take a good look at your image---how you look, sound and act—this the Image Effect. **The Power of Presentation determines how much you can move higher in influence to achieve your goals.**

Question #1:

On a scale from 1 to 10, how sensitive are you to the Power of Presentation?

| 1 | 2 | 3 | 4 | 5 | 6 | 7 | 8 | 9 | 10 |

As a leader, reflect on how you present yourself each day. What two specific ideas can you begin practicing and implementing that will allow your presentation to be more impacting (one-on-one, in small groups, or even in large groups)?

(1) _____

_____

(2) _____

_____

POWER OF ACCOUNTABILITY

It's about honor. It's about getting better. It's about living the right way because it's how to become a better leader.

Accountability is taking responsibility for actions and results. If being accountable was easy, everybody would do it. But it's not. The Power of Accountability is reserved for the few leaders who are willing to grow and become better leaders.

Patrice Lencioni diagnoses a lack of accountability as one of the primary reasons results fail to be exceptional in his book, "The 5 Dysfunctions of a Team". Lack of accountability (4th level of the pyramid) nearly always leads to poor results (5th level of the pyramid). (Lencioni)

Accountability at the Executive Level

The higher a leader goes in an organization, the fewer people there are to hold that leader accountable. The decorated General Petraeus who won the insurgent war in Iraq in 2006 was a man who could do no wrong. Everyone trusted him. He was an American hero.

That is until it was found out that General Petraeus shared top secret information in a scandalous affair with a woman. General Petraeus was forced to retire and face charges.

Good Leaders must learn early to develop the habit of personal accountability so their success doesn't expose their weak character later in life. Accountability is the greatest gift Good Leaders can give themselves as they march through life. **Only Good Leaders are willing to enforce accountability upon themselves for the benefit of themselves and the organization they are with.** Good Leaders will avoid a lot of unnecessary pain and consequences by enforcing accountability upon themselves.

Personal Accountability

The PGA has a tradition of golfers calling penalties on themselves. Strange? Maybe. Hundreds of years since St. Andrews and the founding of this game, everyone competing at the highest levels in the game has been faced with holding themselves accountable when no one is looking.

The New York Times reported the following:

"'It was a very unusual scenario,' [a professional golfer,] McDowell, said, 'where I've got a small branch behind my ball with a leaf attached to it, and in the process of addressing my ball I grazed the top of the leaf, and I'm deemed to have touched a loose impediment in a hazard, which is a two-shot penalty.'"

Another pro-golfer, Peterson, **lost out on a second-place finish** when he incurred a two-stroke penalty for brushing the grass and grazing a leaf during his back-swing when he was hitting out of a lateral water hazard. After finishing tied for third, Peterson said: "It's just one of those things.'" (Crouse)

No one saw either of these events. Only the golfer patrolling himself saw the ball slightly move. **So why call a penalty on yourself that costs you hundreds of thousands of dollars?** Accountability is a way of life for Good Leaders—it's their culture. It's called character, transparency, and ACCOUNTABILITY.

If you cheat here, you will cheat in other places. When will the cheating stop? **Cutting** corners, skimming off the top, telling small lies, etc., destroys the person and the **Good Leader we are working to become.** These failures of accountability may get a leader by for the moment, but they destroy your belief in becoming better the right way.

There are 3 specific things that happen when a Good Leader does not hold themselves accountable:

> 1) They become fake good leaders.
> 2) They look for more shortcuts (because it's easier).
> 3) They lose their zeal & energy to help others become better.

Good Leaders hold themselves accountable because it's the only way to become better in life. To take shortcuts that are not allowed permits leaders to become fake good leaders (pretenders), opportunists for more shortcuts. They become more self-centered, losing their zeal to help others become better.

As the good book says in Numbers 32:23 says, *"and you may be sure that your sin will find you out."*

Today, become a better leader. Decide to be personally accountable for your what you think, say, and do. Your destiny depends upon it.

Question #1:

On a scale from 1 to 10, how well do you, as a leader, hold yourself accountable for your actions and the results?

1	2	3	4	5	6	7	8	9	10

As a leader, what one action-step, above all others, can you take to help you be more self-accountable to the daily promises you make (deadlines, meetings, relationships, etc.)?

_____

_____

POWER OF CONTRIBUTION

Key Word: Contribution - "something that you do to help produce or achieve something, or to help make something successful."

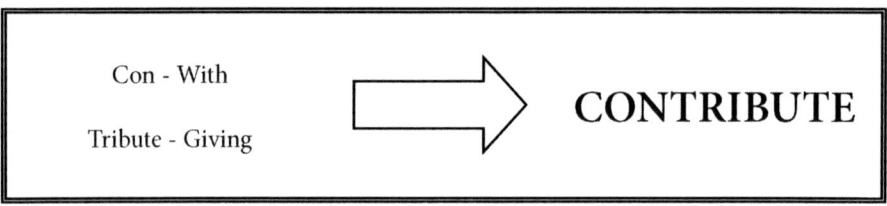

Law of Contribution - What you give when you want to succeed whether it's your energy, time, or money.

Good leaders learn how to get others to contribute to the cause.

Without contribution, there is no emotional ownership stake for the outcome of an event. Leaders want to avoid having unemotional team members. **The greater the contribution, the greater ownership stake there is in the outcome.** Contribution comes in the form of time, energy and money.

It's often called "buy-in." Bankers who loan money want loan recipients to have "skin in the game."

The less you contribute, the less you care about the outcome of an event. **The more you contribute, the greater you will invest your time, energy, and money to a successful outcome.**

Good Leaders can't be successful long-term without getting others to follow their vision. So how does a good leader get others to commit 100% to the vision of that leader's goals?

Answer: **Contribution creates commitment.**

A Good Leader inspires teammates and others to contribute to the vision, goals, and

"Contribution" Def. 1. *Cambridge Dictionary Online*, Cambridge Dictionary, n.d. Web. 2017

outcome of an event. No one in leadership has ever escaped without hearing words like these:

> 1) What's in it for me?
> 2) That seems like an awful lot of work.
> 3) I'm not sure this is worth my time.

The difference between good leaders and average leaders is that good ones know how to get people who ask questions like these to contribute to the vision, goals, and successful outcome. Good Leaders have learned the art of solving people's problems around them. Good leaders understand the power of contribution.

The Power of Contribution creates a commitment in the following ways:

> 1) Emotionally vests the contributor.
> 2) Intellectually vests the contributor.
> 3) Creates a path of significance for the contributor.

Emotional Vesting

Inspiring others for your vision through commitment of time, money, and energy, emotionally captures hearts to want a successful outcome. It means harder work. It means more focused work. It means smarter work, usually.

Leaders who get the greatest Contribution from others do so usually in the following order:

> a) Energy
> b) Time
> c) Money

Energy is often the most difficult of the three resources to secure. Leaders fight to get and keep team members focused and working at a high level toward the vision.

People are protectors of their time. They won't contribute time easily to ideas, people, or visions that don't inspire.

People invest their money. This contribution is important because it focuses the contributors to the success of the vision.

An aspiring leader who consistently inspires others to contribute energy, time, and money will deliver superior results.

Intellectual Vesting

We are rational creatures. We look for ways to put our minds to work. **Good Leaders empower the minds of people around them to contribute to the solutions for the organization.** Good Leaders understand when others are mindfully committed to becoming better, these people are the ones who can help deliver superior performance.

Contributing Significantly

Who contributes the most to an organization? Individuals who see their contributions as significant. **When a leader taps into the significance of others, that leader can deliver superior performance.** Not many things in life deliver commitment as much as those who feel that their contribution is making a significant difference.

What do Good Leaders do that other leaders may not? **They find ways to allow others around them to contribute to the cause, vision, and goals.**

Question #1:

On a scale from 1 to 10, how well do you, as a leader, use the Power of Contribution in getting others to contribute to the cause of the team?

1	2	3	4	5	6	7	8	9	10

Consider a time when you can became frustrated with lack of contribution of a teammate. As a leader, reflect on that moment. What concrete action step could you have implemented to inspire that teammate to contribute better to the team?

_____

_____

POWER OF OWNERSHIP

The "Curse of the Commons" is a phrase used to say no one takes care of what belongs to everybody else. Thomas DiLorenzo writes in "How Capitalism Saved America" about how the pilgrims starved in the early 1600's and failed in establishing colonies initially.

The charter agreement plan that was installed stated that for the first 7 years in the new land, "all profits and benefits that are got by trade, traffic, trucking, working, fishing or any other means of any persons, remain still in the common stock until the division."

With human nature being what it is, nobody wanted to work hard without having some ownership in the business of tilling the field. Heavy winters arrived. People starved. It was brutal.

The finance companies, who had a part in drawing up this contract, saw the error of their ways. They made changes to the contract. They allowed every pilgrim to immediately work and have several acres of land. Whatever the pilgrim could plant he would pay a portion to the commons of the community and the finance company. The rest would be his to sell in the marketplace. Starvation was no longer a problem. Hard work and prosperity were never a problem again because the ownership model was instituted.

If you own, you care. If you don't own, you don't care as much.

Good leaders employ the ownership model in leading others. They do so by getting others to believe that:

1) Vision Matters

2) Each Moment Matters

Vision Matters

Good leaders impart vision constantly. The Scripture says, "Where there is no vision, the people perish."

People that work for you and with you to accomplish goals cannot be their best unless they have a deep sense of who they want to become. Good leaders help others develop this identity and sense of destiny.

Each Moment Matters

Each moment can be rented or owned. The one who rents each moment doesn't care to produce excellence.

Good leaders have a unique ability to get others to take ownership of each moment during the day. How do Good leaders do this?

Good leaders connect where people want to go with their personal vision and solidly tie each moment of the day to that personal vision. **Good leaders inspire others to understand that if others will live by owning the moment, they can achieve visionary heights.**

Only two kinds of people exist. People who rent out each moment---which means those people just get by. **Or people who own each moment, thereby building into their own destiny.** Good leaders inspire others to own each moment so their output is maximized and future is brighter.

Question #1:

On a scale from 1 to 10, how well do others under your leadership employ the Power of Ownership?

| 1 | 2 | 3 | 4 | 5 | 6 | 7 | 8 | 9 | 10 |

As a leader, what two specific ideas could you implement to help others take greater ownership of their schedule?

(1) _____

_____

(2) _____

_____

POWER OF LIFT

Key Word: Lift - "to move something from a lower to a higher position."

Good leaders lift people and circumstances into better places in life. Good leaders practice lifting others out of impoverished circumstances into healthy ones. They take bad circumstances and make better ones out of them. Whether it's distressed companies, conflicted employees, unfortunate circumstances or anything else, good leaders find ways to make life better by solving problems.

Lift Principle: Intentionally living to make the life of everyone and everything in you come across better.

Doing the heavy lifting is not easy. The world is full of personality conflicts. It's full of complex challenges, and seemingly unsolvable problems. **Good leaders, however, see through complexity and the seemingly intractable issues where other people are either emotionally or intellectually overwhelmed.**

How exactly does a Good Leader apply the Lift Principle during painful and confusing circumstances? Leadership lifting requires emotional fortitude and intellectual aptitude.

Emotional Fortitude

There is a good reason why the old adage exists, "People are hired by companies, but people quit people." That's because it's true!

There's a reason why that boss that remains nameless can't keep people around him very long. There's a reason people put resumes out every day instead of growing and developing in one company. There's a reason why divorces are so rampant. In part, it's because there is a lack of emotional fortitude.

Leadership lift begins with the ability to emotionally handle the struggles and trials and difficulties that come with other people's problems. It's deciding to help people

grow through these times instead of constantly discarding people around you because they have problems. **Good leaders have a strong core center that doesn't get sucked into the emotional hurricane of other people's problems.** Instead, good leaders find ways to honestly and genuinely lift others out of their turmoil and help them back onto their path.

Intellectual Aptitude

Good leaders develop the mindful ability to see what's causing problems and find solutions that create win-win outcomes for everyone. Leaders who practice the lifting principle don't run around stomping on others to get ahead. **Instead, Good Leaders find ways to resolve people's problems in a way that improves their condition and outcomes in life.**

But this means taking effort and time to think about others and their circumstances. Then as a good leader, it means producing a solution that may or may not help you. Regardless, Good Leaders are all about helping improve bad circumstances.

To lift others consistently from where they are to higher places in life requires intentional effort on the part of a Good Leader. But no leader can be good if they knowingly leave people behind. That's true for business deals, employment contracts, fellow associates, friends, and marital partners. There is something mysteriously wonderful about Jesus' words: *"So the first will be last and the last will be first."* (Matt. 20:16)

Good leaders recognize this world is not merely about getting ahead in life. **It's about lifting others up and changing the trajectory of their lives as you bring them with you on your journey.** Good Leaders are emotionally and intellectually applying the lift principal so that people are better off because of their presence.

Consider your leadership today. **Are the people around you better off because you consistently apply the Lift Principle?**

For this reason, Good Leaders rise to higher levels in life.

Question #1:

On a scale from 1 to 10, how well do you employ the Power of Lift in leading others?

1	2	3	4	5	6	7	8	9	10

If you could improve using the Power of Lift in other people's lives, what one specific action-step could you take to do so?

_____

_____

POWER OF STORY

Everyone's story is a gift. There is nothing more powerful than telling a story about others as central characters and their successful outcomes.

The difference between two leaders is often the ability to place others at the center of the story being written. One leader may let others be characters in that leader's vision. Another leader authentically shows people how valuable others are in the story that is being written.

Which of the two leaders is likely to create loyalty and deliver superior results?

As a leader, it is your responsibility to paint the story that makes everyone important.

Aspiring leaders who learn the Power of Story:

> 1) Connect - Heart
>
> 2) Teach - Mind
>
> 3) Inspire - Spirit

Connect—Heart

Facts and figures are cold. They don't connect the heart to anything deeper. Stories are about kindling the heart. A good leader introduces the human element of courage, struggle, vision, sacrifice, and inspiration in a story-like manner showing others how they can contribute in a remarkable journey. When a leader authentically empowers others with the belief that they are central figures in a story of becoming successful, that leader forms a strong bond of loyalty.

Teach—Mind

The mind must imagine to become great. If you, as a leader, can connect the heart through the Power of Story, then the mind will begin to imagine. Few things are more powerful than when a good leader authenticates others to believe in "what if."

Leaders who radicalize others with "who I can be," "how far can I go," and "what are my possibilities," create undying loyalty. It's because "what if" makes others a central figure of an important unfolding story.

Inspire—Spirit

Telling people how valuable they are in the story of your vision is what good leaders excel at. A good story inspires. It elevates. It takes the "what if" to a place of executing the game plan.

How well do you tell a story? The organization you work for and the people you work with are desperate to give their lives to a story that matters.

How much can you make the story of those around you matter in the vision you have as a leader?

Question #1:

On a scale from 1 to 10, how well do you employ the Power of Story in other people's lives?

| 1 | 2 | 3 | 4 | 5 | 6 | 7 | 8 | 9 | 10 |

What two specific strategies can you, as a leader, employ to improve in telling the story about other people's lives?

(1) _____

_____

(2) _____

_____

POWER OF NEW BEGINNINGS

Good leaders take advantage of the Power of New Beginnings.

There are two kinds of New Beginnings in life:

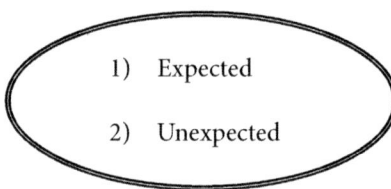

Unexpected New Beginning

Be Prepared - that's the motto of the Boy Scouts.

"Be prepared for what?" someone once asked Baden-Powell, the founder of Scouting.

"Why, for any old thing," said Baden-Powell.

Prepare for the unexpected.

When Peyton Manning injured his neck as quarterback of the Indianapolis Colts then missing the entire 2011 season, a new quarterback was installed in his place. Manning would never play quarterback for the Colts again. After 14 years of blood, guts, and loyalty, Peyton Manning's injury seemed to shut the door on him. The Colts let him go from the team.

It's not how he would've written the story. But Manning saw the "Power of New Beginning". At age 35, when professional athletes tend to retire, Manning worked harder than ever to make a comeback. He rehabilitated his neck. He cut a deal to play with the Denver Broncos in 2012. Manning led the Broncos to 4 Division Titles in a row. In 2015, Manning took the team to the Super Bowl and retired on his own terms.

It's not how Peyton Manning wanted the story to go. In fact, it was a sentimental nightmare. But he turned the unexpected into the Power of New Beginnings.

Good leaders don't let events that are out of their control destroy who they are becoming. New beginnings are about coming face-to-face with who we are deep down and what we want to do. **New beginnings challenge our current situation, our imagination, and our strength to overcome adversity.**

Expected New Beginning

In ancient Israel when Rehoboam, King Solomon's son, was born, this young lad expected to become King of Israel. He had the greatest opportunity for preparation. When his father died and Rehoboam became king, he was ill-prepared to fill this powerful position.

Rehoboam did the unthinkable. His leadership split the twelve tribes apart which became the northern and southern kingdoms.

Good leaders prepare, anticipate, and capitalize on Expected New Beginnings. Don't be like Rehoboam whose New Beginning became a failure because he didn't prepare well.

Why do some leaders fail in their opportunities for advancement? **Poor leaders don't mentally, emotionally, or spirituality prepare well for New Beginnings.** Good Leaders are empowered by the Power of New Beginnings to be impacting.

New Beginnings bring 3 specific changes to most Good Leaders:

>1) Summons Courage
>2) Brings Humility
>3) Kindles Creativity

Summons Courage

Will you have courage to step into the new season of your life? Courage is having the fortitude to overcome fear. New Beginnings have risk. **The leader who gathers courage to face the risk of the New Beginnings can grow.** Fear of New Beginnings limits the capacity of a leader to grow. New Beginnings summon courage to apply the hard lessons you have learned, which are full of sweat and tears, to this new venture.

Brings Humility

New Beginnings force us to take stock of who we are--our talents, our virtues, and our character. Where have we gone wrong? What are our strengths? What can we do to improve who we are? The Power of New Beginnings brings a fresh humility to the new season.

Without humility, we cannot grow as leaders. A leader can still make money. They can still receive awards. **But they cannot grow as a person or significantly as a leader apart from humility.** Humility means having a reflective spirit that searches that person's heart.

Kindles Creativity

The Power of New Beginnings opens up amazing possibilities about who you are and what you can do. **This principle compels a Good leader to create, grow, and develop into the next level and season of life.** To move to the next challenge, whether expected or unexpected, can be uncomfortable. But New Beginnings, which make us squirm and give us butterflies in the stomach, are also the ones that bring us alive to become who we want to become.

Question #1:

On a scale from 1 to 10, how well do you use the power of New Beginnings?

| 1 | 2 | 3 | 4 | 5 | 6 | 7 | 8 | 9 | 10 |

Describe what specifically you can do to improve your approach to New Beginnings in your life:

_____

_____

POWER OF CELEBRATION

As a leader, learn to celebrate well. Give credit. Give honor. Share the glory of successful achievement with those around you who have earned it. Good leaders who do this create undying loyalty and greater hunger for further success.

Good leaders never underestimate the Power of Celebration. **The Power of Celebration changes the way people think about who they are, why they are here, and where they are going under your leadership.** Good Leaders choose to celebrate others and their achievements. By pointing to the unique remarkable accomplishments of others born of courage, discipline, and fortitude, Good Leaders win hearts and minds.

Celebrating others is one of the highest honors a leader can use to develop the destiny of others. The Power of Celebration plays a vital role in three specific ways:

> 1) Affirms Significance
> 2) Inspires Vision
> 3) Establishes Momentum

Affirms Significance

Good leaders affirm how valuable others are to the cause or the vision. The Power of Celebration allows leaders to extol the well-deserved virtues and results of team members. In so doing, this affirmation brings a positional and cultural significance to those being celebrated for their achievement. **Those being affirmed by a Good Leader find a home and a resting place they can trust to continue growing.**

Inspires Vision

Celebrating victory inspires greater vision. Victory is intoxicating. It elevates confidence. The Power of Celebration allows those who have achieved success to think bigger and higher than before.

St. Matthew, in the Scriptures, records a powerful story (Matt. 25:14-30) told by Jesus to teach a lesson. Three men were given talents to invest. One was given 5 talents, another 2 talents, another 1 talent. The individuals with five talents and two talents went out, risked their investment, and doubled their investment. The one with a single talent buried his talent in the ground for fear of failure.

Which of these men should we celebrate and honor for their courage, discipline, and fortitude to deliver superior results? Jesus said that the man with one talent not only wasted this talent, but that this man's talent would be stripped of him. There will be no celebration of this man's future or achievements. This man creates no value for those around him.

Good Leaders will wildly celebrate the successes of others so that others can be inspired to expand and grow further into further victories. Good Leaders use the Power of Celebration to inspire others into greater vision.

Establishes Momentum

The power of celebration creates momentum. Every organization has ebbs and flows to it. Not every day is about sunshine and roses, but every day has purpose. When enough days string together to create victory, a Good Leader then knows to use the Power of Celebration to multiply the existing momentum to further heights. **Celebration creates new energy, abundant satisfaction, and sustainable confidence that individuals and team members are winning and on the right path to further victory.**

Remember that the leader who does not celebrate the victory of others lessens morale and easily loses team members. But those leaders who go out of their way using the power of celebration to celebrate the achievement of others will create an environment of success.

POWER OF YOU

Good Leaders find ways to honor the victory of others using the Power of Celebration. The Power of Celebration, when employed well, affirms significance, inspires vision, and creates momentum for further victories.

Question #1:

On a scale from 1 to 10, how well do you use the Power of Celebration to celebrate the achievement of others around you?

1	2	3	4	5	6	7	8	9	10

What one specific concrete step could you take, as a leader, to improve your ability to celebrate the achievements of those around you?

_____

_____

POWER OF HEALING

Key Word: Healing - "the process of becoming healthy or whole again."

What does a Good Leader have to do with the Power of Healing? Everything.

Brokenness is everywhere. It's in marriages, families, work relationships, partners, schools, etc. Psychologists and psychiatrists are busier than ever trying to fix people's lives. Life coaches have exploded on the scene guiding successful career-minded people through their pain and brokenness.

Good Leaders are good because they are agents who facilitate the Power of Healing in the lives of people. They don't walk past the pain of others.

Saint Paul declares, *"The Father of Compassion and the God of all comfort who comforts us in all our troubles (is given to us), so that we can comfort those in any trouble with the comfort we ourselves have received from God."* (2 Cor. 1:3-4)

Good Leaders meet hurt, distress, and the dejection of others with unique care, influence, and wisdom. **Good Leaders facilitate the Power of Healing where there is brokenness.**

The Power of Healing is about being an instrument that helps meet the needs of others in their trials of life. Good Leaders don't leave the hard work to priests and pastors and social workers. Good Leaders passionately learn how and why people think and act as they do. Good Leaders become instrumental in the Power of Healing by doing three things well:

> 1) Listen
> 2) Empathize
> 3) Care

Listen

Good Leaders don't have to be professional counselors. But a Good Leader listens well. They don't interrupt. They connect with others. Good leaders are *"quick to listen, slow to speak and slow to become angry."* (James 1:19)

Only a Good Leader takes a genuine interest in the outcome of each person around them. They first listen with their eyes and ears. They wait to talk. Listening is an art form. Listening well is difficult to do for leaders who care about getting ahead in their life but don't have a significant desire to see people around them improve and advance in life.

Empathize Well

Good Leaders don't argue with others. The goal is to help others become sound or healthy. Arguing destroys the bridge of trust that a Good Leader wants to build.

"Reckless words pierce like a sword, but the tongue of the wise brings healing." (Prov. 12:18)

Good Leaders learn how to place themselves in the position of that other person. **Nothing builds trust faster or better than someone else knowing that you, as a Good Leader, feel their pain and struggle.**

Care Well

To care is to act well. **The golden rule of care is to do what needs to be done when it's needed.** People struggle physically, emotionally, mentally, and spiritually. Good Leaders find ways to help meet these needs. The Power of Healing is helping others become sound and healthy again. To care well is to invest in others in a way that propels others to places they couldn't get alone.

In the Scriptures, Timothy writes to those who have the ability:

"Command them to do good, to be rich in good deeds, and to be generous and willing to share. In this way they will lay up treasure for themselves as a firm foundation for the

coming age, so that they may take hold of the life that is truly life." (I Tim. 6:18-19)

Good Leaders facilitate healing. They treat those around them with dignity and a uniqueness that allows others to live with soundness and health.

As a leader, are people around you becoming more sound and healthier? Aspire to listen well, empathize well, and care well. In doing so, you will bring the Power of Healing into people's lives.

Question #1:

On a scale from 1 to 10, how much is your presence one of healing in the lives of others?

1	2	3	4	5	6	7	8	9	10

What one specific action-step, as a leader, can you take to help improve your ability to have a healing presence in the lives of others?

_____

_____

CONCLUSION

How do we tackle the existing leadership deficit found in our politics, businesses, churches, and marriages?

Good leadership is grounded in the many habits found in the *Power of You*. Leaders who listen, reflect, and fight to build better character become uncommonly good leaders. The timeless values in this book, beginning with the Power of Early to the Power of Healing, is a reminder that leaders have power to grow in wisdom and improve life for everyone around them.

What are the factors that often stifles leaders from becoming all they can be? First, when a leader does not purposefully invest enough time to reflect on who they want to become, that leader hits a glass ceiling both personally and professionally. Without investing time to intentionally grow, a leader is bound to become ineffective. The rotting of good character soon follows a leader who does not regularly churn the soil of the mind and heart. Greater leadership is highly correlated to a commitment to read, think, and write. These are the essentials for growing.

Secondly, we should note that reflection is a soulful activity that develops self-awareness. The 49 concepts in this book provides a time of reflection to be self-aware and improve personally and professionally. Reflection is a leader's way to measure the correctness and wisdom of actions amid complicated circumstances. Most complications in life arise from a failure to detect the timeless values that govern good decision-making. Through persistent reflection, a leader will strengthen the better part of one's thinking and resolve.

The clarion call of this book, *Power of You*, asserts that leaders who embrace virtue and good character are uniquely set apart to win in this culture. The difference between leaders who succeed at the highest level versus others is determined by how well they employ the superior habits described in this book. It is through good habits that leaders become effective agents of change in our culture.

NOTE FROM THE AUTHOR

I want to personally thank you for reading *'Power of You.'* I am deeply humbled by anyone who worked their way though the concepts of this book on the road to building good character. I have produced a list of powerful books that can help churn the soil of your mind as well.

1. How to Win Friends and Influence People by Dale Carnegie
2. The 7 Habits of Highly Effective People by Stephen Covey
3. Do You Have What It Takes? by Walter Nusbaum
4. Think and Grow Rich by Napolean Hill
5. The Five Levels of Leadership by John Maxwell
6. The Art of Strategy (1988) by R.L. Wing
7. Imagine That by James Maples
8. The Little Engine that Could (Original-1930) by Watty Piper
9. Happiness is a Choice by Frank Minirth & Paul Meier
10. Focus by Daniel Goleman
11. Grit by Angela Duckworth
12. Talent Code by Daniel Coyle

BIBLIOGRAPHY

Pg 23, 28 - "Understanding" Def. 1 & 4. *http://dictionary.cambridge.org.* Cambridge Dictionary, 2017. Web. (n.d.)

Pg 37 - "Victory" Def. 1. *http://dictionary.cambridge.org.* Cambridge Dictionary, 2017. Web. (n.d.)

Pg 49 - "Radical" Def. 2. *http://dictionary.cambridge.org.* Cambridge Dictionary, 2017. Web. (n.d.)

Pg 58 - "Desire" Def. 1. *http://dictionary.cambridge.org.* Cambridge Dictionary, 2017. Web. (n.d.)

Pg 60 - "Execution" Def. 1. *http://dictionary.cambridge.org.* Cambridge Dictionary, 2017. Web. (n.d.)

Pg 66 - "Precision" Def. 1. *http://dictionary.cambridge.org.* Cambridge Dictionary, 2017. Web. (n.d.)

Pg 68 - "Transformation" Def. 1. *http://dictionary.cambridge.org.* Cambridge Dictionary, 2017. Web. (n.d.)

Pg 86 - "Optimism" Def. 1. *http://dictionary.cambridge.org.* Cambridge Dictionary, 2017. Web. (n.d.)

Pg 97 - "Habit" Def. 1. *http://dictionary.cambridge.org.* Cambridge Dictionary, 2017. Web. (n.d.)

Pg 121 - "Decision" Def. 1. *http://dictionary.cambridge.org.* Cambridge Dictionary, 2017. Web. (n.d.)

Pg 124 - "Presentation" Def. 1. *http://dictionary.cambridge.org.* Cambridge Dictionary, 2017. Web. (n.d.)

Pg 128 - Lencioni, Patrick. *The Five Dysfunctions of a Team: A Leadership Fable*, San Francisco: Jossey-Bass, 2002.

Pg 129 - Crouse, Karen. *"In Golf, Rules Are Rules. Even the "Stupid" Rules."* New York Times, 10 Sept. 2012. Web.

Pg 132 - "Contribution" Def. 1. *http://dictionary.cambridge.org.* Cambridge Dictionary, 2017. Web. (n.d.)

Pg 136 - DiLorenzo, Thomas. *How Capitalism Saved America: The Untold History of Our Country, from the Pilgrims to the Present*, Crown Forum, 2005.

Pg 139 - "Lift" Def. 1. *http://dictionary.cambridge.org.* Cambridge Dictionary, 2017. Web. (n.d.)

Pg 144 - Birkby, Robert. *Boy Scouts Handbook. 11th ed (#33105),* Empire Books, 1998.

Pg 151 - "Healing" Def. 1. *http://dictionary.cambridge.org.* Cambridge Dictionary, 2017. Web. (n.d.)

Back Cover - "Leadership" Def. 1. *http://dictionary.cambridge.org.* Cambridge Dictionary, 2017. Web. (n.d.)